Nelson Mandela

Nelson Mandela

Laaren Brown &
Lenny Hort

DK Publishing

LONDON, NEW YORK, MUNICH,
MELBOURNE, AND DELHI

Editors : John Searcy, Alisha Niehaus

Publishing Director : Beth Sutinis

Senior Designer : Tai Blanche

Art Director : Dirk Kaufman

Photo Research : Anne Burns Images

Production : Ivor Parker

DTP Designer : Kathy Farias

First American Edition, 2006

13 10 9 8 7

009-DD346-Jul/2006

Published in the United States
by DK Publishing
345 Hudson Street, New York, New York 10014

DK books are available at special discounts for bulk purchases for
sales promotions, premiums, fund-raising, or educational use.
For details, contact:
DK Publishing Special Markets
345 Hudson Street, New York, New York 10014
SpecialSales@dk.com

Library of Congress Cataloging-in-Publication Data

Brown, Laaren.
  Nelson Mandela / Laaren Brown & Lenny Hort. -- 1st American
ed.
    p. cm. -- (DK biography)
  Includes bibliographical references and index.
  ISBN-10 0-7566-2109-7 ISBN-13 978-0-7566-2109-4 (pbk.) --
ISBN-10 0-7566-2110-0 ISBN-13 978-0-7566-2110-0
(hardcover)
  1. Mandela, Nelson, 1918---Juvenile literature. 2. Presidents--
South Africa--Biography--Juvenile literature. I. Hort, Lenny. II.
Title. III. Series.
  DT1974.P37 2006
  968.06'5092--dc22
  [B]
                                   2006006772

Color reproduction by GRB Editrice, Italy
Printed and bound in China by
South China Printing Co., Ltd.

Photography credits:
Front cover: David Turnley/Corbis
Back cover: Paul Gilham/Getty Images

Discover more at
www.dk.com

Contents

chapter 1

A Troublemaker Is Born

In a tiny village in southern Africa, on the banks of the Mbashe River, in the district of Umtata, in the Thembu royal house, a new baby was born. He came into a world that had remained unchanged for many years. Yet in his lifetime, this baby, this boy, this man, would see changes undreamed of by his ancestors.

Eventually he would be called Nelson Mandela, and he would lead his people to freedom. But today, July 18, 1918, this new baby was called Rolihlahla. In Xhosa, the language spoken by his family, Rolihlahla meant "pulling the branch of a tree" but everyone understood that it really meant "troublemaker." Nelson Mandela was destined to become one of the

Rolihlahla's family lived in traditional Xhosa huts much like these.

greatest troublemakers in the history of the world.

Transkei, where Rolihlahla lived, was home to many blacks. His family had a tradition of leadership. His father was a chief, both because he was born to the role and because he was approved by the king of the Thembu tribe—one of many in the Xhosa nation—and the local head of the British government that ruled South Africa.

By Xhosa custom, cousins were raised as brothers and sisters, and a father's wives acted as mothers to all his children.

Rolihlahla's father, Chief Gadla Henry Mphakayisa, had four wives. Like the other wives, his mother, Nosekeni Fanny, had her own *kraal,* a home with a hut, a fenced-in area for animals, and fields. But when Rolihlahla was still a little boy, his father lost his chieftainship by refusing to appear before the local British judge on a minor dispute.

"My father possessed a proud rebelliousness, a stubborn sense of fairness, that I recognize in myself," wrote the grown Mandela. By refusing to appear in court, Chief Henry was telling the magistrate that, as a Thembu chief, he was not governed by the laws of England. The magistrate angrily took away Chief Henry's job and title. His family immediately lost

their money, land, and livestock. Suddenly poor, Rolihlahla and his mother moved to Qunu, a village where she had friends and family. His father visited their mud hut one week each month.

Nelson Mandela grew up in Transkei, but he spent his working life in Johannesburg, and most of his long prison life at Robben Island.

His life was simple and spare, but Mandela loved Qunu. He thought of the rugged but beautiful countryside as his true home for the rest of his life. He was surrounded by family—and in the tradition of his tribe, the children of his aunts and uncles were considered not his cousins, but his brothers and sisters. The boys spent hours playing in the veld, or grasslands, then returned home to hear exciting stories of Xhosa warriors.

Young Nelson Mandela's happy rural boyhood was much like the boyhoods of generations of Xhosa boys. But the way in which his father lost his home and his livelihood symbolized the problems of South Africa. Even in 1918,

BOER

A Boer is a South African of Dutch descent, but the term has been replaced by "Afrikaner."

when Rolihlahla was born, the country had serious problems with relations between the native Africans and the whites who had come to the country.

8

Many white people in South Africa are descended from Dutch and English merchants who had first come to the Cape of Good Hope when it was a stop on the spice trading route to India and the Far East. By the mid-1600s, the Dutch, or Boers, had established a colony that was eventually called Cape Town.

By the 19th century, the British had captured the Cape from the Dutch. Meanwhile, the Xhosa, who lived on the eastern edge of the land populated by the British and Dutch, were gradually driven back by the whites, just as Native Americans were driven out of their traditional lands in the United States. And, as in the U.S., the newly arrived South African colonists had skirmishes with different tribes for many years. But a big difference between South Africa and the U.S. was that in South Africa, the white Europeans never outnumbered the native peoples. They were always a small minority.

In this 1804 picture, a Boer hunter returns to his lavish home, accompanied by his African servants.

Then, in the late 1800s, South Africa was suddenly transformed by the discovery of diamonds and gold. Suddenly this dry, barren land was hugely valuable. The white population exploded as immigrants rushed to take control of the mines. Railroads were built with incredible speed. South Africa exploded onto the international economic scene; it soon supplied about a third of the world's gold and half of its diamonds.

Who worked the mines? Black Africans. Men came from the countryside to find work in the mines around the city of Johannesburg. The whites got richer off the labor of the blacks, who earned barely enough to survive. By the time Rolihlahla was a boy, Qunu was a village made up entirely of women and children. The men were all off working in the mines.

Nelson Mandela grew up in this simple hut in Qunu. Today it is a museum.

Influenced by friends, and probably hoping for a better future for young Rolihlahla, Chief Henry did something no one in his family had ever done. He sent his son to the local one-room school, run by missionaries. Seven-year-old Rolihlahla had special clothes for school: a pair of his father's pants, cut down and tied with a string around the boy's waist. "I must have been a comical sight," wrote Mandela later, "but I have never owned a suit I was prouder to wear than my father's cut-off pants." On the first day of school, the teacher gave every child an English name. On that day, Rolihlahla became Nelson.

Nelson, a hard worker, quickly picked up the basics of a solid British-style education. Nothing about his own culture was ever taught in the white-run schools. Then one afternoon he came home from school to find his father lying on the floor, coughing violently. A few days later, silent and still proud, Chief Henry died.

The family mourned. Then Nelson's mother gathered his few possessions and took him on a long, long walk, until they reached the most elegant home the boy had ever seen—two buildings and seven huts, all whitewashed, surrounded by orchards, corn fields, sheep, and goats. This was the Great Place, capital of Thembuland and home of Chief Jongintaba Dalindyebo, leader of the Thembu people. Long before, Nelson's father had helped the chief, and now the chief had volunteered to take charge of Nelson's upbringing. Jongintaba became Nelson's friend, mentor, and guardian, raising him in the Great Place with his own children.

chapter 2

Growing Up

To Nelson, the Great Place was "a magical kingdom." Even his mother's departure could not dampen his spirits; he rode horses, shot birds with slingshots, herded sheep, and danced and sang. His favorite job was ironing the chief's six Western-style suits, making the crease in the pants sharp as a knife (and beginning a lifelong love affair with fine clothes). He went to school in a hut next to the palace.

Chief Jongintaba's leadership influenced Mandela for the rest of his life.

His classmates were the other children of the family, although Jongintaba's son Justice was at boarding school. Justice was four years older than Nelson and was the younger boy's idol—handsome, extroverted, and excellent at sports.

Nelson was learning a great deal—not because he was unusually smart, but because he was hardworking and observant. Perhaps the most important thing he learned at the Great Place was leadership. He watched Jongintaba during tribal meetings, when Thembu people would appear before the chief to present their sides in disagreements. Jongintaba

12

would listen in silence. Then, at the end of the day, when all arguments had been made, he would make a decision. By the custom of the

CIRCUMCISION

Circumcision is the removal of the foreskin of the penis.

Thembu, the chief's decision represented a consensus. Jongintaba heard all the evidence and came up with a solution that respected the interests of everyone involved.

Watching and listening at the chief's side, Nelson Mandela heard it all. In his adult life, consensus building would be a hallmark of his leadership. A leader should be like a shepherd, Jongintaba told him: "If one or two animals stray," he said, "you go out and draw them back to the flock. That's an important lesson in politics."

In 1934, 16-year-old Nelson and twenty-five other Thembu boys, including Justice, were taken to a quiet valley to attend bush school, a series of rituals that would guide the boys on their final steps into manhood. At the end of their studies, they were circumcised in an ancient ceremony that symbolized their new status.

Afterward, a special ceremony welcomed the 26 new men into adulthood. The honored speaker of the day, Chief Meligqili, congratulated them. Then his

After circumcision, new Xhosa men are painted with white ocher to symbolize their purity.

message darkened: "We have [promised them] manhood, but I am here to tell you that it is an empty, illusory promise, a promise that can never be fulfilled. We are slaves in our own country. . . . [These men] will cough their lungs out deep in the bowels of the white man's mines, destroying their health, never seeing the sun. . . . The abilities, the intelligence, the promise of these young men will be squandered in their attempt to eke out a living doing the simplest, most mindless chores for the white man."

This is the first picture ever taken of Nelson Mandela. He was 19 years old.

A silence fell over the crowd. Everyone, including Nelson Mandela, was shocked by the chief's attitude toward whites. But in the months that followed, Mandela began to understand the chief's message: "He had planted a seed, and though I let that seed lie dormant for a long season, it eventually began to grow."

For now, though, Nelson was to be educated at a white man's school. Chief Jongintaba drove him to Clarkebury Boarding Institute. The young man thought he would be a star at school, but he quickly realized that "most of my classmates could outrun me on the playing field and outthink me in the classroom."

14

Still, his hard work helped him graduate from Clarkebury in two years rather than the usual three. At 19, Nelson joined Justice at his new school, Healdtown. With more than 1,000 students from all over the country, Healdtown was big and cosmopolitan. But it was still very much part of South Africa: Whites and blacks did not intermingle.

In Mandela's last year at Healdtown, a renowned Xhosa poet, Krune Mqhayi, appeared at the school wearing a leopard-skin *kaross,* the traditional cloak of the Xhosa. His words were as memorable as his clothing: "We cannot allow these foreigners who do not care for our culture to take over our nation . . . for too long, we have succumbed to the false gods of the white man. But we will emerge!"

"I had many new and sometimes conflicting ideas in my head," said Mandela. Where did he fit in, as a Xhosa, as an African, as a young black man being educated by whites? Why did blacks allow whites to control their country?

With feelings of unrest, Mandela left Healdtown to begin his studies at the South African Native College at Fort Hare, the only black university in South Africa. He joined about 200 other students: many Xhosa, others from other places and tribes, plus Indians, Coloureds (people of mixed race), a few women, and even a handful of whites. Fort Hare was a hotbed of political discussion. One of Mandela's best friends there was K.D. Matanzima, his own nephew from the Thembu royal family. Much later, they would oppose each other politically, but for now they were young men full of ideas and dreams.

15

Mandela had a common touch and friends from every background, but he also had a regal dignity that made people respect him. Tall, good-looking, and athletic—he ran cross-country, played soccer, and boxed—he stood out among the students. Secretly, though, he marveled at the new things he was seeing at Fort Hare: pajamas, toothbrushes and toothpaste, flush toilets, showers with hot water, even bar soap (at home everyone washed with blue detergent).

When Jan Smuts visited, Mandela discovered that Smuts's English was almost as bad as his own.

The most important friend Mandela made during his years at Fort Hare was Oliver Tambo, who would later become his law partner and closest associate. Tambo was already involved in politics, and Mandela was not. When Jan Smuts, soon to be the prime minister of South Africa, spoke at Fort Hare to gain support for South Africa's entry into World War II on the Allied side, Mandela applauded his ideals of world freedom, even as

Fewer than 200 students were attending Fort Hare in 1939, when Mandela started there.

the government denied blacks freedom in their own country.

In his second year at Fort Hare, Mandela was elected to the student government—but

BOYCOTT

A boycott takes place when a group of people refuses to take part in an activity in an effort to bring about change.

only 25 students actually voted. Most had boycotted the vote, demanding better food in the cafeteria. Since they had not been elected by a majority, Mandela and the five other winners of the election resigned. In new elections, the same small number of students voted, and the same six students won. The other winners agreed to serve despite the flawed elections, but Mandela—as principled and proud as his father had been when he defied the British magistrate—refused. The principal—as stubborn as the magistrate—expelled him.

Back home at the Great Place, Chief Jongintaba was furious. In poor health and eager to settle the family line, he had arranged marriages for both Mandela and Justice. Mandela knew the young woman who was intended for him. "I would be dishonest if I said that the girl was . . . my dream bride," said Mandela. *And* she was in love with Justice! Justice didn't like the wife Jongintaba had selected for him, either.

The young men's lives were at a turning point. Should they follow the path of marriage and a safe life? Or should they choose adventure and strike their own path? They made their decision. They ran away—to Johannesburg, the city of gold.

17

chapter 3

Joining the Fight

Johannesburg was the big city, and Nelson and Justice were dazzled. They arrived with thousands of other young black men from the country. Like most of the others, Nelson and Justice looked for work in the nearby gold mines.

Afrikaners, the white South Africans of Dutch descent, were frightened by the number of black Africans moving into the city and called the migration "the black peril." Some called for *apartheid*, the word for "separateness" in Afrikaans, the Afrikaner language. In many ways, Johannesburg was already separate. Even the mines were segregated, with separate housing and facilities for black workers.

PLAYLAWN
FOR EUROPEAN INFANTS
ONLY

SPEELVELD
ALLEEN VIR BLANKE
BABAS

Even before apartheid
became government policy,
racism was everywhere.

Tribal chiefs often sent men to work in the mines, and, before their falling out, Jongintaba had arranged for Justice to be hired as a clerk. Not realizing that his father now wanted him home, the headman gave Justice the job. Mandela got a job, too, patrolling the grounds as a security guard. As soon as Jongintaba tracked the pair down, however, he made sure they both got fired. Justice was eventually hauled home, but Nelson wanted to stay in the city. He got a tip that Walter Sisulu, a businessman, might be able to help.

Apartheid

Apartheid separated blacks and whites in South Africa long before the National Party made it law in the early 1950s. Throughout the country, there were already separate facilities for blacks and whites, including separate schools, restaurants, water fountains, and bathrooms. Sometimes the "Native" facilities were labeled, much like "Negro" facilities in the American South. Sometimes everyone just followed unspoken rules about which things were for blacks, and which were for whites.

Sisulu, short, energetic, and brilliant, was to become Mandela's lifelong friend and political ally. Born in Transkei like Mandela, he had been a cowherd and a gold miner, a dishwasher and a factory worker. When Mandela arrived on his doorstep, Sisulu saw the young man's potential instantly. "I marked him at once as a man with great qualities, who was destined to play an important part," said Sisulu.

Sisulu helped Mandela get a job as an articled clerk (an apprentice to a lawyer), and Mandela found a cheap place to stay in Alexandra, a black slum. Often called the Dark City, Alexandra had no electricity, and the night was full of frightening noises: screams, laughter, and even gunfire. Mandela commuted to work, six miles each way on the "Native" bus, for Africans only, when he had the money. Some days he walked.

The lawyers' office treated blacks as "equally" as any place in Johannesburg, and yet on Mandela's first day, a white secretary told him they had purchased new tea cups "in honor of your arrival . . . for you and Gaur." Gaur Radebe was the only other African in the office. Mandela knew that the "new cups" were the secretaries' way of making sure that they would never drink tea from a black man's cup. Radebe said, "Nelson, at teatime, don't worry about anything. Just do as I do."

Walter Sisulu's activism inspired Mandela to become more politically involved.

When the tea arrived, Radebe, ignoring the sparkling new cups, carefully selected an old cup. Milk, sugar, hot tea—he stirred slowly, then drank. The white secretaries stared in horrified silence.

Mandela said, "I'm not thirsty."

Soon he would become more confrontational.

Sisulu and Radebe, troublemakers both, were already active in the struggle for African rights. In the evenings, Radebe was working to establish a mineworkers' union. With others all around him working to improve conditions, Mandela was becoming more politically aware. When Radebe organized a bus boycott to protest a fare hike, Mandela marched with more than 10,000 blacks. The "Natives," despite their desperate need for the buses, boycotted for nine days. At last, the fares were lowered. Excited by this victory for nonviolent protest, Mandela joined the African National Congress, a political group which Sisulu and Radebe already belonged to.

"I cannot pinpoint a moment when I became politicized . . . but a steady accumulation of a thousand slights, a thousand indignities, a

In tent cities outside Johannesburg, the poorest blacks were crowded into makeshift huts.

Dr. Alfred Xuma

Born in Transkei, Alfred Xuma became, through luck and hard work, a medical doctor, educated in the U.S. and Europe. Brilliant and energetic, he was elected president of the ANC in 1940 and quickly revived the group, making it into a real force on the South African political scene. But he was conservative compared to the men who came later. The ANC Youth League was created despite his opposition to "my kindergarten boys" and their plans for mass action.

thousand unremembered moments, produced in me an anger, a rebelliousness, a desire to fight the system that imprisoned my people," he wrote later.

Founded in 1912, the ANC had started as a conservative group, rarely opposing white leaders. Only now, in the early 1940s, under the leadership of Dr. Alfred Xuma, was the group beginning to challenge racism. With Walter Sisulu and Anton Lembede, a Zulu activist, Mandela formed the ANC Youth League in 1944. The Youth League brought the young men of the ANC together—often to challenge the staid leadership of the main ANC.

While Mandela worked by day and organized in the evenings, he also completed his college degree through a correspondence course, studying by candlelight late into the night. After he received his degree, Mandela moved to Orlando, a planned community for "the better class of Native." Sisulu lived nearby with his mother and his wife, Albertina.

Mandela needed the more peaceful environment in order to study for his law degree. He was one of the very few black students at Johannesburg's University of Witwatersrand. There he was treated with casual cruelty: When he sat down in class, white students moved away, and he was frequently called a "kaffir," a racial slur. Despite the hardships, Mandela attended "Wits" from 1943 to 1949, but he had little time for his studies. He asked his professor if he could rewrite some of his papers, explaining that he usually

Evelyn, a cousin of Walter Sisulu's, was a quiet girl from the country.

did not arrive home from work until late in the evening, tired and hungry. "If I could have done my work under more suitable conditions, I would have produced better results," he said. The professor said no. Mandela left the school without his degree.

He was also distracted from his studies by another cause. Handsome, athletic, and ambitious, he said, "I can't help it if the ladies take note of me. I'm not going to protest." But soon he had settled on just one lady, Evelyn Mase. In 1944, Nelson and Evelyn were married. Pretty, sweet Evelyn was not interested in politics, just in keeping

CONSERVATIVES

Conservatives tend to avoid social change. Liberals aim to make changes in society.

a nice home for her busy husband—who was becoming more and more active in the struggle for freedom.

chapter 4

Working for Unity

The Mandelas had a happy home. After a year of marriage, their son, Thembi, was born. Nelson's mother arrived to help with Thembi and soon a new baby girl, Makaziwe. Mandela was a devoted father, playing with the babies, giving baths, and putting them to bed. But tragedy struck the little household when Makaziwe passed away at only nine months old.

Grieving, Mandela threw himself into politics. In the early years after World War II, the idealistic young men of the ANC Youth League felt that conditions would soon improve in South Africa. The British and Americans and their allies—including South Africa—had just fought against the discrimination of Nazi Germany, hadn't they? Now that the war was over, wouldn't these powers realize that there was persecution and racism right here in South Africa?

South Africa's Communist Party also hoped for civil rights for blacks. Mandela wrote that communists were the only whites who "were prepared to treat Africans as human beings and their equals; who were prepared to eat with us, talk with us, live with us, and work with us." Communists were eager to work with the ANC, and so were

24

organizations of South African residents originally from India. South Africa had hundreds of thousands of Indian workers. Like

COMMUNISM

In the political system called communism, all companies that produce goods or services are owned by the people as a group.

blacks, most worked at unskilled jobs, and all faced constant discrimination. Even Coloured people—those of mixed race— were considered "lower" than whites, but "higher" than blacks.

Unfortunately, South Africa's ruling United Party would not use its power to solve the problem of racism. This was obvious barely a year after the end of the war, when Gaur Radebe's new African Mineworkers' Union organized a strike. More than 70,000 black miners demanded better working conditions and pay. The government, led by Jan Smuts, allowed the mining companies to use bayonets to force the miners back to the mines. Nine men were killed, and hundreds more were injured.

Thousands upon thousands of black laborers worked in South Africa's mines, under terrible conditions.

25

Indians were treated just as poorly. A proposed law would make it illegal to sell land to Indians. Under the new law, all Indians would be forced to live on land that was already Indian-owned—or wherever the government told them to go. Angry, yet inspired by the nonviolent protests led by Mohandas Gandhi, Indians protested by occupying and picketing land reserved for whites. Over a period of two years, some 2,000 protesters went to jail.

Dr. Yusuf Dadoo led Indians in nonviolent protests against the South African government.

In 1947, the Indian groups and the ANC created the Doctors' Pact, named after Dr. Alfred Xuma, and Dr. Monty Naicker and Dr. Yusuf Dadoo, leaders of the Indian resistance. The pact agreed that the ANC and two Indian groups would work together for a free South Africa. Mandela worried that the concerns of black Africans would be lost among the problems faced by the Indians. He worried that communists would take over the ANC and follow their own political agenda. Mainly he worried that time was passing, and South Africa seemed no closer to equality for its black citizens.

Mandela was now the secretary of the ANC Youth League. He often debated political ideas with Sisulu, Tambo, and his other friends in the organization. Mandela always said, "Loyalty to an organization takes precedence over loyalty to an individual." Despite his doubts about some of the ANC's decisions, he was convinced that it was the only group that could build a consensus among people, in the spirit of Jongintaba and his tribal leadership, and win freedom for all.

In 1947, the British royal family visited South Africa. Smuts enforced a clear color barrier wherever the family went. King George VI, father of the future Queen Elizabeth II, was told not to shake the hand of any black leader. Yet crowds of cheering blacks greeted the family wherever they went. What message did these crowds send? Probably that

Mandela, Gandhi, and Nehru

Mandela admired Indian activists for their resilience and persistence. He met with their leaders, including Ahmed Kathrada, who introduced him to the teachings of Mohandas Gandhi and Jawaharlal Nehru. Gandhi championed the principles of passive resistance, leading nonviolent protest against British rule in India. Mandela was impressed by the way Gandhi's commitment to nonviolence led directly to real change in India, which gained independence in 1947. But he felt more kinship with Nehru, who was willing to push back against oppressors.

Mohandas Gandhi

Jawaharlal Nehru

most black people were happy with the current British-backed rule and the way they were treated. The ANC boycotted the celebrations.

But soon Smuts and his British-based government were gone. In their place came an even more antiblack government. The National Party, supported by many Afrikaners, won the elections of 1948, running on a platform of strict apartheid. The apartheid of the Nationalists meant new rules and new laws that boiled down to white

The British royal family was greeted by cheering blacks wherever they went—but they traveled in an all-white train.

supremacy. "From the moment of the Nationalists' election, we knew that our land would henceforth be a place of tension and strife," Mandela said.

NATIONALISM

Nationalism is a belief that one's nation is better than all others.

Culturally, Afrikaners, descended from the Dutch Boers, were very different from the English-speaking British residents of the country. This new election victory offered Afrikaners their chance to claim South Africa as their own after decades of British rule. They were nationalistic, and so were black South Africans. Mandela knew that "both nationalisms laid claim to the same piece of earth—our common home, South Africa," and that "the contest between them was bound to be both heated and brutal."

Despite violent riots, the National Party's new prime minister, Daniel Malan, quickly established harsh new laws. Every person in the country would be classified by race. Each race would live in separate parts of the cities. Marriages between people of different races would be illegal.

The ANC Youth League demanded action, but the leadership of the larger, more conservative ANC wanted to avoid provoking the government. When Xuma resigned as president of the group in 1949, Mandela, Tambo, and other members of the Youth League were elected to the ANC's national executive committee, and Sisulu became the ANC's new secretary-general. Mandela was pleased. At last the ANC was ready to exert pressure on the authorities. It was ready to fight.

chapter 5

Acts of Defiance

In the slums of Johannesburg, where thousands upon thousands of blacks were crowded, everyone hoped that the Nationalist government would soon be gone. Nelson Mandela, finally starting to make some money from practicing law, was spending it on nice suits and good meals in city restaurants—that is, the few restaurants that would serve blacks. To stay in shape, he boxed for 90 minutes every weekday.

Mandela often used his regal presence to make a stir at political meetings. At one meeting where communists focused on using the economy of South Africa to overthrow apartheid, Mandela put the problem to the crowd in simpler terms: "There are two bulls in this kraal. There is a black bull and a white bull. [Communists] say that the white bull must rule this kraal. I say that the black bull must rule. What do you say?" The people screamed back, "The black bull, the black bull!"

The rise of Daniel Malan and his Nationalist government was a cause for concern even in the United States.

Despite their tense relationship with communists, the ANC Youth League was impressed by their May Day protest in

MAY DAY

May Day is a celebration of workers, observed by communists and many others around the world on May 1 every year.

1950, when more than half of Johannesburg's black workers stayed at home. Walking home that night, Mandela and Sisulu spotted a peaceful demonstration—and mounted policemen approaching. The officers beat protesters with nightsticks. Then they began shooting. The next morning, 18 blacks were dead.

"That day was a turning point in my life," Mandela later said. For the first time, he had seen the brutality of the police up close. And for the first time, he realized that masses of African workers would respond to calls for protest.

Mandela spars with South African boxing champion Jerry Moloi.

So when the communists organized to protest the newly proposed Suppression of Communism Act, Nelson Mandela and the ANC supported them. The ANC proposed a "Day of Mourning" strike, organized by Mandela, with workers staying home on June 26, 1950.

But this strike was a failure. Few stayed home, and those who protested faced harsh treatment from the police. The law passed, and the Communist Party in South Africa officially dissolved. Left behind, however, were plenty of communists, all looking for a group that would help them organize against the National Party. Most joined the ANC. Mandela had once opposed the communists; now, in the spirit of consensus, he welcomed them into the ANC fold.

Meanwhile, the government's policies were growing tighter, and oppressive laws were introduced. Now black men were required to carry passes wherever they went—papers that would show their identity and make it easy to track where any individual had gone or was going. The Group Areas Act forced different racial groups to live in specific areas. The Bantu Authorities Act dictated

By law, black men were required to carry passes wherever they went and to show them on demand.

a separate, limited education for blacks so, the government explained, they wouldn't "aspire to positions they would not be able to hold in society." And the Suppression of Communism Act meant not only that communists couldn't meet in public places—it meant that no political groups could, and that included the ANC.

At the ANC's 1951 congress, Walter Sisulu presented plans for a huge civil disobedience campaign known as the Defiance Campaign. With Gandhi-style passive resistance, people would defy the new laws, even if it meant going to prison.

The Defiance Campaign rallied thousands of people to protest apartheid.

Plans moved ahead quickly. In January 1952, ANC leaders sent a letter to Prime Minister Malan, demanding that the new laws be repealed. If they were not, the Defiance Campaign would begin on June 26. On June 22, with the laws still in place, Nelson Mandela spoke to a crowd of 10,000 people—a group far, far larger than any he had addressed before. In an inspiring speech, he told his listeners that the Defiance Campaign signaled a dawn of new hope for South Africa, and would be a powerful movement that

DEFIANCE

Defiance is the act of fighting or challenging an action or statement.

33

In one of the many acts of civil disobedience during the Defiance Campaign, blacks took over a whites-only train car.

united blacks, whites, Indians, and Coloureds in the name of freedom.

The Defiance Campaign began on schedule. Mandela went to Boksburg, where hundreds of supporters with green, black, and gold ANC armbands waited for him. As demonstrators entered the township through the big gates—without the passes demanded by the government—Mandela looked on, calm and majestic.

The police were waiting inside the gates. Most of the leaders were bundled into vans and taken to the closest prison. This was expected; one of the goals of the campaign was to challenge the government by overburdening the prison system.

Mandela himself soon had his first jail experience. That night he traveled back to Johannesburg to appear at a late meeting. The gathering was peaceful, but before Mandela

34

could speak, the police arrested everyone. Mandela spent two nights in the dirty, overcrowded jail, pressed against other protesters. One man fell and broke his ankle; the police let him scream in pain all night long.

Mandela was shocked, but the experience had toughened him. Like his fellow protesters, he had lost his fear of jail. "From the Defiance Campaign onward, going to prison became a badge of honor among Africans," he said. In the next five months, more than 8,000 people were arrested.

Shockingly, the Defiance Campaign only made the government more determined. Police raided the ANC offices and campaign leaders' homes. The government banned Mandela from holding office in the ANC, but he was elected president of the Youth League anyway. Then it banned 52 ANC leaders, including Mandela, from attending any meeting, even from talking to more than one person at a time.

In some ways the Defiance Campaign had succeeded: It brought the struggle for freedom to many, many more people, showing them that they could be part of the fight. In other ways it had failed: The government used it to fan the flames of fear among whites that they would be overrun by blacks, Indians, communists, and Coloureds.

Perhaps the most meaningful result of the Defiance Campaign was that it firmly established the ANC as the most important protest group in South Africa—and at the same time, it established Nelson Mandela as one of the great leaders of that protest.

chapter 6

The Revolutionary and the Lawyer

At home, the great protester was a settled married man. Evelyn minded the children and ran the household. To outsiders, it looked very cozy. But the marriage was no longer happy. While Nelson became more and more involved with politics, Evelyn became more and more involved with her religion. Many nights the two argued.

Meanwhile, in addition to his political efforts, Mandela had a demanding career as a lawyer. After finishing his apprenticeship, he worked for a series of white-owned firms. Mandela had failed to earn his law degree at Wits, but there was another way to earn the right to practice law: a written exam. With a passing score on the exam, he was

As young lawyers, Mandela and Tambo "heard and saw the thousands of humiliations that ordinary Africans confronted every day of their lives."

ready to help poor Africans who had no one else to turn to. In 1952, with Oliver Tambo as his partner, he opened the first-ever black law firm in South Africa.

Mandela's friendship with Tambo had deepened since their days at Fort Hare. Tambo was quiet and bookish, a counterpoint to Mandela's bold charisma. He too was involved in politics. Business was brisk at Mandela and Tambo. All the new laws meant that Africans were constantly breaking the law, sometimes whether they meant to or not. Mandela and Tambo were greeted each morning by a new crowd of blacks looking for fair treatment.

Compassionate, patient Oliver Tambo worked tirelessly with clients.

Bold Mandela was the one who usually appeared in court. In the courtroom, he quickly acquired a reputation for being "uppity," for entering through whites-only doors, and for challenging racism.

In 1954, after the Defiance Campaign had ended and Mandela had received a suspended sentence for organizing it, the board overseeing the country's lawyers sued to end Mandela's law career. He won the case. But the walls were closing in. Mandela could practice law, but he couldn't travel outside Johannesburg to do so. He was also forbidden from

37

SUSPENDED SENTENCE

Under a suspended sentence, a person does not have to serve prison time if he obeys the law for the length of his sentence.

making speeches in public, from holding public office, and from working with the ANC. Isolated from his friends and fellow activists, Mandela quickly began to feel like a hunted criminal—a feeling that was reinforced by the policemen who followed him wherever he went.

The other members of the ANC were having similar problems, and their isolation threatened the freedom movement. To help the ANC work around the roadblocks constructed by the government, Mandela created the M-Plan—named after himself without using his name, since that would have revealed that he was violating his bans and working with the ANC.

The M-Plan allowed ANC leaders to send secret messages. The system could be used directly for ANC needs, or to assist labor unions and other groups that could not hold public meetings without attracting the attention of the police.

Mandela wanted to work within ANC policies, but he was feeling more than ever that "nonviolence was not the answer." In Sophiatown, the only section of Johannesburg where blacks were allowed to own property, residents were being forced out of their homes in exchange for tiny government "compensations." Mandela led a protest in Sophiatown right after his bans ended in June 1953. The crowd was angry, and he was almost unable to control his own anger. "There are our enemies!" he sang in one ANC song as he pointed to police.

Ultimately, nonviolence failed: On February 9, 1955, with more than 2,000 policemen patrolling the area, government trucks removed the last tenants of Sophiatown while ANC members watched helplessly.

By destroying Sophiatown, the government destroyed an important part of black South African culture.

Mandela saw that nonviolence was ineffective against a violent government. In December 1953, he told a crowd in Soweto, "We have to employ new methods in our struggle. It is no longer sufficient to speak from platforms. . . . You will not shed blood in vain."

Still the consensus builder, Mandela embarked on a new project: helping to compile a Freedom Charter that would express the beliefs of the ANC and the people it represented. By now he was convinced that the way forward was to cooperate with Africans of every political and racial stripe—with everyone who was willing to offer assistance.

Throughout the country, hundreds of meetings were

BANS

Bans were a way to control activists by prohibiting them from public speaking, leaving an area, or engaging in various other acts.

39

held to brainstorm ideas for the Freedom Charter. The poorest of the poor spoke on "tens of thousands of scraps of paper [that] came flooding in: a mixture of smooth writing-pad paper, torn pages from ink-blotched school exercise books, bits of cardboard, asymmetrical portions of brown and white paper bags, and even the unprinted margins of bits of newspaper," one of the activists remembered. At last those with no voice were able to speak.

Mandela, Sisulu, and many others worked together on the final document, which was to have a unique role in history. Echoing the American Constitution, it began: "We, the people of South Africa, declare for all our country and the world to know: That South Africa belongs to all who live in it, black and white, and

More than 3,000 people gathered to hear the Freedom Charter read aloud—but police were standing by.

that no government can justly claim authority unless it is based on the will of the people."

The final document was presented at the Congress of the People on June 26, 1955. A true cross-section of South Africans met, more than 3,000 people from every walk of life. The gathering of so many people, united, was inspiring—but Mandela was uneasy. Why had the huge meeting been allowed to proceed? Police surrounded the field in Soweto but did not interfere.

Mandela, in disguise because he was once again under a ban, watched as the charter was read aloud in three different languages and the crowd responded with cries of "Afrika!" On the second day, the charter was to be approved by the people. Section by section went by until the words "there shall be peace and friendship" were read. As if on a signal, armed policemen darted into the crowd. One seized the microphone and shouted that they were investigating high treason at the event.

Eventually, June 26 became a South African day of celebration, Freedom Day. But at the time, the raid signaled a harsh new turn. Now the government was actively cracking down on demonstrations rather than simply hobbling activists with bans.

The ANC's worst fears about the government were coming true. Instead of loosening apartheid, the Nationalists were tightening the policy with terrifying speed. Malan retired and was replaced by the even more pro-apartheid

Hans Strijdom. Soon Strijdom's minister of native affairs, Hendrik Verwoerd, came up with harsh new plans to separate blacks from whites completely. Mandela called them "Verwoerd's Grim Plot."

Meanwhile, after 15 years in Johannesburg, Mandela longed to see his childhood home and his family. Now, in September 1955, his bans momentarily lifted, he went home to Transkei. He visited partly to relive pleasant memories and partly to fight the Bantu Authorities Act. This new law was designed to trick tribal chiefs into feeling more important among their people, while actually moving tribes even more firmly under the government's thumb. Under the law, all tribal leaders would actually be paid by the government—and so the government would be free to fire them at will.

Mandela's mother greeted him with joy. She lived alone, plowing her own

CAUTION BEWARE OF NATIVES

Signs like this were common in Johannesburg.

fields, a strong peasant woman who had encouraged her son to fight for what he believed in. Mandela also went to see an old friend from Fort Hare, his nephew K.D. Matanzima. Matanzima, now the chief of Western Thembuland, was in favor of the Bantu Authorities Act. Mandela warned him that the law would be used to weaken

Tribal chiefs

Throughout South Africa, different areas are home to specific tribes—for example, the Xhosa live in the south and the Zulu in the east. Tribes are led by chiefs, or tribal leaders; Jongintaba was a tribal leader of the Xhosa. The South African government sometimes manipulated tribal leaders to gain control of the people they led or the land they owned.

black unity, ultimately leading to bloodshed. Matanzima was family, but he was on the other side of the fence politically. He said that apartheid would strengthen the authority of tribal leaders and that "equality" among the races would only encourage fighting between them. Mandela was deeply saddened that he and his old friend felt so differently.

He continued his Transkei trip, meeting Govan Mbeki, a leader of the Eastern Cape ANC. Then he went on to Cape Town, sightseeing along the way. Mandela returned home with a clearer picture of how weak the ANC really was in the countryside. Outside the big cities, was anyone fighting for an end to apartheid? It would take many long years to persuade the people outside Johannesburg and Cape Town to join the struggle.

chapter 7

Treason?

Early on December 5, 1956, Nelson Mandela was arrested. The charge: high treason. He wasn't the only one. The police arrested 156 anti-apartheid leaders, black, white, Indian, and Coloured. The roundup was the final piece in the government's plan to remove the opposition.

Mandela tried to joke with the police officers who came to get him. They weren't laughing. "You are playing with fire," one told him.

"Playing with fire is my game," he snapped back.

The police made all the captives strip naked in order to embarrass them. Even respected older men like Chief Albert Luthuli, a distinguished Zulu tribal leader, stood naked in the outdoor holding area. One of the prisoners began to recite a traditional song about Shaka, the mighty Zulu warrior of the early 1800s. Inspired, the men sang and danced to the flowing words and rhythm. They felt "bound together by love of [their] history," Mandela later remembered.

Within days, the men realized that there was opportunity even in jail. All of

Albert Luthuli "combined an air of humility with deep-seated confidence," wrote Mandela.

44

them had been under bans for so long that this was the first meeting they had been permitted to attend in years! They quickly organized lectures and discussion groups to exchange ideas.

After two weeks, the accused were taken to hear the charges. The indictment was 18,000 words long, about the length of this book. The accusations were based on statements

Shaka

Shaka, a Zulu warrior, led his armies from 1812 until 1828, when he was killed by his half brothers. A ruthless man but a great military strategist, Shaka introduced new weapons and battle plans and enlarged his army by adding warriors from conquered tribes to his own Zulu troops. The larger army, aided by Shaka's military innovations, was able to hold Europeans back from the Zulu homeland for many years.

the men had made as long as four years before, during the Defiance Campaign, right through the protests in Sophiatown and the Freedom Charter congress. The statements, said the prosecution, revealed that the men were trying to overthrow the South African government using violence in order to replace it with a communist state.

Did the government really think the Freedom Charter and other inspirational documents were treasonous? Mandela considered. Probably not. The trial was just the latest idea to

INDICTMENT

An indictment is the written document formally charging a person with a specific crime.

keep the activists down for a while. Little did any of them realize that "a while" would turn into five years in court.

45

BAIL

Bail is money paid to temporarily release a prisoner from jail.

After a few days in prison, the captives were freed on bail. Mandela arrived home to discover that Evelyn had left him. At the heart of their troubles was their disagreement about religion versus politics. "Her faith taught passivity and submissiveness in the face of oppression, something I could not accept," said Mandela. Their children—Thembi, Makgatho (a son born in 1950), and Makaziwe (a little girl born just two years before and named after the child they had lost)—were caught in the middle.

Nelson's arrest was the last straw. Evelyn had taken the children and everything else, right down to the curtains. Nelson stood alone in the empty house, silent and shattered.

Hearings began in January 1957. These preliminaries alone took more than nine months. The whole first month was taken up by cataloging the piles of evidence the government had assembled to prove its accusations, from a United Nations Declaration of Human Rights to a Russian cookbook. Then there were

On the first day of the trial, the accused file into the courthouse. Mandela is the third man from the front.

several months when policemen, many barely able to read and write, described scenes they had supposedly witnessed at ANC gatherings. One officer claimed to remember whole sections from ANC speeches he had heard years earlier, but the lines he "remembered" were complete gibberish. Joe Slovo, one of the accused, was acting as his own lawyer.

He asked the officer, "Do you understand English?"

"Not so well," said the witness.

"Do you agree that your notes are a lot of rubbish?" asked Slovo, later.

"I don't know," admitted the officer. The defendants started laughing. The judge cautioned them, saying, "The proceedings are not as funny as they may seem."

Joe Slovo

Joe Slovo was one of the heroes of the anti-apartheid movement. Born in Lithuania, he joined the South African Communist Party at 16, eventually becoming the group's leader. White, Jewish, and a lawyer, he was a defendant at the Treason Trial and worked side by side with black activists for decades. When he died in 1995, Mandela said, "In his life there was only one target . . . to remove the racist regime and obtain power for the people."

Outside the trial, protesters and police clashed, as the proceedings became the focal point of the freedom movement.

As the hearings dragged on, respect was building among the activists. "We didn't realize we had so much in common," said one Indian leader. Together, the men ate lunch and talked; in the evenings, they went to parties and talked more.

Mandela, newly single, also socialized outside the group. Then, driving one day, he spied a beautiful young woman waiting for a bus. He drove on, but he couldn't get her striking face out of his mind.

A few weeks later, he was at work when Tambo was visited on a legal matter by a young woman and her brother. Nelson recognized her as the girl from the bus stop. Her name was Nomzamo Winifred Madikizela, but everyone called her Winnie. She came from Pondoland, in Transkei, and she was one of the first black female social workers in South Africa. Nelson could not concentrate on the law. "I cannot say for certain if there is such a thing as love at first sight," he wrote, "but I do know that the moment I first glimpsed Winnie Nomzamo, I knew that I wanted to have her as my wife. Her spirit, her

Nelson never actually asked Winnie to marry him. Instead, he told her where to go to buy a wedding dress.

passion, her youth, her courage, her willfulness—I felt all of these things the moment I first saw her."

Nelson embarked on a lightning-fast courtship. Winnie agreed to marry him, but her family was not pleased. Nelson was 16 years older than Winnie, who was just 22. He was well respected, true, but he was a known troublemaker and he was already on trial. How long would he be able to avoid prison? "My sisters literally cried," Winnie said later. They begged her not to marry him, but marry him she did, on June 14, 1958. At her family's party, her father warned her that Mandela was married to his politics, and that she must join him: "If your man is a wizard, you must become a witch."

Soon she had made the transformation. Back in Johannesburg, Winnie rapidly established her own political life. At a meeting designed to teach public speaking to black women, she cried, "I don't think we need to be taught how to speak. From our suffering we can just tell people how we feel."

After a huge antipass march in Pretoria, Winnie was charged with inciting other women to not carry passes. When a policeman tried to arrest her, she knocked him to the floor. In October 1958, a pregnant Winnie insisted on attending a Johannesburg rally, where she was arrested and jailed. "I've married trouble!" moaned Nelson.

The Treason Trial moved on. In December 1957, the judge ruled that the case should go to the Supreme Court, and Mandela realized that he could be looking at jail time. His defense was weakened by a split in the ANC between the newly emerging Africanists and the established group leadership, including Mandela and Sisulu. Africanists did not believe in the core idea of the Freedom Charter, that there was room for everyone in South Africa, if only everyone could be treated fairly. The Africanists wanted to use violence in order to take over the country.

Like many other men, Nelson Mandela burned his pass after the Sharpeville Massacre.

Eventually the Africanists created the Pan Africanist Congress, their own political party, and elected Robert Sobukwe as its president. The PAC and the ANC began organizing rival antipass demonstrations. Typically, the ANC planned and planned, and PAC depended on last-minute support. Sobukwe's plans: "In every city, town, and village, the men must leave their passes at home." Men should simply go to the police and surrender.

Surprisingly, many did. In Cape Town, where support for PAC was strong, 1,500 men went to police stations and asked to be arrested. More protestors gathered around the station. Trying to break up the crowd, the police fired and killed two demonstrators. This was tragedy enough—but on March 21, 1960, in the township of Sharpeville, thousands of people

MASSACRE

A massacre is the killing of a large number of defenseless people.

surrounded the police station. By the afternoon, when the crowd had dwindled to a few hundred, the police opened fire, killing 69 demonstrators and injuring 300 more, in what would forever be called the Sharpeville Massacre.

Suddenly South Africa's troubles were international news, and around the world, its government was criticized. The economy weakened, and whites applied for visas to move to other countries in record numbers. ANC leaders, including Mandela, burned their passes. The government, momentarily cowed, announced that it would not be arresting people for traveling without passes. The tide seemed to be turning.

On March 30, the PAC led 30,000 people in a march in Cape Town. To end it, the government promised the protest leader a meeting with the minister of justice—then, after the leader had sent the protestors home, he was tossed

After the massacre, the bodies of protesters lay on the ground outside the police station.

into jail. He had been tricked. It was the end of the government's hesitation. More than 2,000 people were arrested, including Mandela. No more passes were burned. In fact, people began applying for replacements.

After years in Johannesburg, the Treason Trial moved to a synagogue in Pretoria.

During all this, the Treason Trial continued in Pretoria. At last it was time for Nelson Mandela himself to testify. His evidence was especially important because his bans had prevented him from speaking publicly for so long.

Mandela's testimony began with a statement in which he explained how, at first, he had favored African nationalism—that is, keeping South Africa strictly for blacks—but had come to believe that all races should live peacefully together in South Africa. During questioning, he talked about how the ANC had refused to encourage violence.

52

While the trial dragged on, the ANC smuggled Oliver Tambo out of the country. For the next 30 years, he would serve as Mandela's "man on the outside"—both outside South Africa and, later, outside Mandela's prison world. Their law practice had collapsed. Mandela rarely saw Winnie or their two daughters, Zeni and Zindzi. His life was a mess, and the government showed no signs of giving any rights to blacks.

Mandela organized one more meeting, the Maritzburg Conference, held on March 22, 1961, and attended by 1,400 representatives from 145 different South African groups. His ban ran out just before the conference, so Mandela was able to appear at the meeting's close—the first time he had made a speech outside a courtroom since 1952. The crowd was astounded and delighted to see him. "Africans must feel, act, and speak in one voice," he said. The air rang with cries of *"Amandla! Ngawethu!"* ("Power to the people!"). Mandela left quickly. He did not appear in public again for almost 30 years.

At last a verdict was declared in the Treason Trial: not guilty. The defendants lifted their lawyers onto their shoulders and danced; Mandela was happy, but he knew that the government oppression would continue, worse than before because this trap had failed.

And so he disappeared.

During the Treason Trial, Mandela consulted with Sisulu (left) and another defendant.

chapter 8

The Black Pimpernel

Nelson Mandela went underground. The ANC needed more supporters, and it would be Mandela's job to find them—a job that was almost impossible when he was under a ban.

He never went home after the Treason Trial. Instead he became invisible—although, he said later, "This is not much of an adaptation for a black man in South Africa." He stooped. He mumbled. He passed as a "garden boy" or a chauffeur. A black man driving his own car was sure to be noticed—but a chauffeur, driving his master's car, would be ignored.

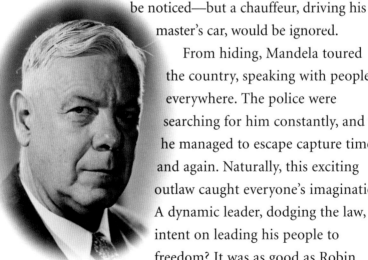

From hiding, Mandela toured the country, speaking with people everywhere. The police were searching for him constantly, and yet he managed to escape capture time and again. Naturally, this exciting outlaw caught everyone's imagination. A dynamic leader, dodging the law, intent on leading his people to freedom? It was as good as Robin Hood—better! The press dubbed him "the Black Pimpernel" after the

Hendrik Verwoerd was the force behind apartheid for many years.

dashing hero of the novel *The Scarlet Pimpernel.*

Even Mandela was caught up in his act. He called newspaper reporters from pay phones. When they answered, he would drop hints about what the ANC was planning or how the police had managed to let him slip through their fingers once again.

He had some narrow escapes, though. One day,

The Scarlet Pimpernel

The Scarlet Pimpernel, star of a 1905 novel by Emmuska Orczy, was a superhero before there were superheroes. In everyday life, he was Sir Percy Blakeney. But he had a secret identity—the bold Scarlet Pimpernel, who saved rich people from the guillotine during the French Revolution. Unlike Mandela, he didn't help the poor and downtrodden. The press probably just liked the sound of "the Black Pimpernel"—and Mandela liked it, too.

stopped at a light, he turned and saw the local police chief in the car next to him. "The seconds I spent waiting for the light to change seemed like hours," remembered Mandela, but the officer never even looked at him. He was invisible, after all.

Mandela organized a stay-at-home strike for May 29, 1961. Hendrik Verwoerd, now the prime minister, threatened drastic action against anyone who supported the strike, using armored vehicles and armed soldiers to show

UNDERGROUND

A person who goes underground is in hiding and operates outside the official establishment.

what he meant. On the second day, Mandela called it off, meeting with reporters to tell them, "If the government reaction is to crush by naked force our nonviolent

55

"The struggle is my life. I will continue fighting for freedom until the end of my days."

—Nelson Mandela, to the press

struggle, we will have to reconsider our tactics." It was time to fight fire with fire—or, as Mandela put it in Xhosa, *"Sebatana ha se bokwe ka diatla,"* meaning "The attacks of the wild beast cannot be averted with only bare hands."

The Treason Trial, in which Mandela and the other defendants had spoken of their commitment to nonviolence, was barely behind them. But the conditions in South Africa had gotten much worse. Mandela convinced the ANC to let him form a separate military organization. Although the ANC would still have an official policy of nonviolence, the reality was that Mandela and his allies were embarking on a new and more dangerous path.

Mandela's new group, Umkhonto we Sizwe, the Spear of the Nation, was called MK for short. He hardly knew where to begin; he had never been a soldier or fired a gun at another person. With Joe Slovo and Walter Sisulu, Mandela studied guerilla warfare and sabotage, the tactics "least violent to individuals but most damaging to the state." In a letter to newspapers, he wrote, "Only through hardship, sacrifice, and militant action can freedom be won. The struggle is my life. I will continue fighting for freedom until the end of my days."

Still on the run, Mandela hid in a white area. But he gave himself away. He liked amasi, soured milk. One day, after placing the milk on his window ledge to sour, he overheard two young black men talking. "Amasi," said one in Zulu. "What is it doing there?" It was clear what the man meant: In this white neighborhood, who would make a black person's food?

Mandela moved to Lilliesleaf Farm in Rivonia, a suburb of Johannesburg. The ANC had bought the farmhouse to give shelter to underground activists. Soon members of MK were coming and going; Winnie and the children even came to visit.

But Mandela was not there to rest. On December 16, 1961, MK struck, setting off homemade bombs at power plants and government offices in Johannesburg, Port Elizabeth, and Durban. Two weeks later, another set of explosions went off, and the government started a manhunt to capture members of MK. Meanwhile, Mandela left the country to attend the Pan African Freedom Conference in Addis Ababa,

Guerilla warfare

Around the world, guerilla warfare is waged by groups with few resources against more powerful armies. During the American Revolution, the American army was a ragtag bunch compared to the well-trained professional British soldiers. Yet the Americans won the war—with guerilla tactics such as small, quick strikes against the enemy. MK's plans emphasized sabotage: destructive acts designed to harm buildings, disrupt services, and weaken military forces without injuring people.

Ethiopia, and to make several stops in other countries to gather support for the ANC.

Mandela (far left), with his beard and khakis, trained at the Algerian Military Headquarters in 1962.

Once he had made it out of South Africa—no easy feat—he stopped for a meeting in Tanzania, then traveled to Ghana, where he was reunited with Oliver Tambo. Together the former law partners made their way to the conference in Addis Ababa, where Mandela spoke about the oppressive South African government and the ongoing sabotage campaign. (He did not mention that he was the leader of MK.) But the ANC had not abandoned nonviolent tactics such as strikes and demonstrations, he said: "We will resort to them over and over again."

58

In Oujda, Morocco, near the Algerian border, Mandela learned guerrilla warfare tactics from Algerian freedom fighters. Then he continued on his travels, stopping in London. South African friends exiled there begged him to stay. The police would surely capture him at home. "Why go back?" they asked.

"A leader stays with his people," said Mandela simply.

Back in Africa, Mandela stopped in Ethiopia for arms training. He finally returned to Lilliesleaf Farm early on July 24, 1962, and the ANC held a meeting there that night. He left soon after to consult with Chief Luthuli. To travel, Mandela drove the same new car that had carried him back into South Africa—a big mistake, since it was easy to spot. On his way home, he got pulled over by the police. They had been tipped off.

Soon he appeared in court, where, perhaps for the first time, he realized that he had become larger than life. "I was the symbol of justice in the court of the oppressor, the representative of the great ideals of freedom, fairness, and democracy," he said later.

An arrest warrant for Mandela was issued on May 18, 1961.

Mandela was charged with inciting workers to strike and with leaving the country without a passport. Acting as his own lawyer, he appeared in court in a Xhosa leopard-skin kaross, tossed across his shoulders like a cloak, "literally carrying on my back the history, culture, and heritage of my people." (Perhaps he remembered the sensation the poet Krune Mqhayi had made in a kaross at Healdtown so many years before.) He concluded his defense with an hour-long political statement.

Winnie attended the trial that last day, in Pondo tribal dress. She and dozens of other Africans heard Mandela speak of his dreams of a peaceful, free land in an inspiring speech. But he was still sentenced to five years in prison, the harshest penalty South Africa had ever given for a political offense.

Mandela was proud of his tribal heritage.

Nelson Mandela, the crusading lawyer, the Black Pimpernel, the ANC leader, had sacrificed everything for his cause. He had become a martyr.

So, in 1962, Nelson Mandela disappeared again—this time into the prison at Pretoria. He immediately complained about the prisoners' uniform of short pants—humiliating for a grown man. Punished with solitary confinement, he realized that he needed people around him. Alone, his mind created its own torture:

"There is no end and no beginning; there is only one's own mind, which can begin to play tricks. Was that a dream or did it really happen?"

Mandela stayed at the Pretoria prison for six months, assigned to sewing dirty, bug-infested mailbags. Then one day he was handcuffed to three other prisoners and driven to a boat docked in Cape Town. Mandela and the other prisoners were forced to stand belowdecks as guards urinated on them from a porthole above. When the boat stopped, the guards shouted, *"Dis die Eiland! Hier julle gaan vrek!"*—"This is the island! Here you will die!"

Robben Island

Wild, beautiful Robben Island has been used to house convicts, lepers, and the mentally ill for more than 400 years. The first political prisoners arrived in the 18th century, black men who the Dutch called "Indiaanen bandieten," or local bandits. By the 1850s, the prisoners included Xhosa warriors who had revolted against British rule. In 1960, the island—used most recently as a World War II stronghold—was made into a jail specifically for political prisoners.

Robben Island, like San Francisco's Alcatraz, was an especially feared prison. Eight miles (13 kilometers) of cold, dangerous water separate it from the mainland, making escape next to impossible. Starting in the 1950s, it mostly housed political prisoners.

61

Sitting in his cell that first evening, after a day of cruelty and abuse, Mandela heard a voice calling him from the window: "Nelson, come here." A Coloured guard gave him a message from Winnie, plus cigarettes and food. Mandela was comforted to know that even in the worst places on earth, there were still kind people.

A few weeks of hard labor passed, and then Mandela was sent back to Pretoria. At first, he couldn't understand why. Then, in the prison office, he saw Walter Sisulu, Ahmed Kathrada, and Govan Mbeki. They were among the ANC leaders who had been hiding at Lilliesleaf Farm in Rivonia. The farm had been raided in July 1963, and the government had found everything. Everything, including many documents that revealed the ANC's plans for sabotage and guerrilla warfare. Everything, including dozens of papers in Mandela's handwriting, notes from the leader of MK. Everything.

The penalty could be death.

As far away as Cambridge, England, Mandela's supporters were spreading the word of his imprisonment.

Mandela entered the courtroom, thin and pale from months in jail. But then he raised his right fist in a salute and cried "Amandla!" to the people in the courthouse. "Power!"

"*Ngawethu!*" answered the blacks: "The power is ours!"

When asked for his plea, Mandela said, "It is not I, but the government, that should be in the dock. I plead not guilty."

As the prosecutor read the charges—among them organizing

Winnie Mandela showed amazing strength throughout her husband's trials.

MK and planning more than 200 acts of sabotage—the lawyers for Mandela and the other ANC leaders despaired. "Was there any hope whatever that any of the accused would escape the death sentence?" thought one.

Paper after paper condemned the men and revealed their sabotage work. One, labeled "Strictly Confidential," discussed antipass activities and ended with "This document should not fall into wrong hands. Study it and understand it. Then destroy it in the presence of, at least, two other comrades." Yet there it was in the courtroom, bearing witness to ANC plans.

If all of these papers weren't enough to convict the accused men, one of the ANC saboteurs appeared as a

63

witness—for the government. Bruno Mtolo
identified Mandela as the leader of MK and
described how he had spoken of sabotage.
It was the last piece of evidence the
government needed to convict.

Mandela's lawyers found him
inspiring throughout the trial:
brave, forthright, and pleasant,
even in the face of death. In his
final statement, read just before
the verdict was to be announced,
he concluded, "During my
lifetime, I have dedicated myself
to this struggle of the African
people. I have fought against white
domination, and I have fought against
black domination. I have cherished
the ideal of a democratic and free

Outside the Rivonia
courtroom, Mandela's
mother (right) and his
daughter Zindzi waited
for the judgment.

society in which all persons live together in harmony with
equal opportunities. It is an ideal which I hope to live for
and achieve." His voice dropped. "But if needs be, it is an
ideal for which I am prepared to die." There was a long
silence. Then, together, the people in the audience sighed,
as if they had been listening to a beautiful piece of music.

The court was adjourned for three weeks, the verdict to
be announced on June 11, 1964. On the night of June 10,
Mandela wrote tidily numbered notes to himself on what

he would say if he was sentenced to death. Number two: "I meant everything I said."

Assembled in the courtroom, the accused waited for the verdict. The judge spoke: All the major defendants were guilty on all counts. The sentence would be announced the next day.

On June 12, the convicted men gathered in the courtroom for the last time. Winnie, strong as ever, and Nelson's mother were waiting there. At last the judge spoke. He would not give the men the supreme penalty. Someone in the crowd gasped with joy. But he was sentencing them to life in prison.

It was a harsh sentence, but Mandela smiled. He would live. The fight for freedom would go on.

Passionate demonstrators in Pretoria protested Mandela's life sentence.

chapter 9

Life on the Island

Nelson Mandela is a unique figure in history. If you ask people about him, they might say, "Oh, he spent years and years in prison." In a strange way, Nelson Mandela became a great leader because he was in prison for 27 years. Looking at his life before he went to jail, it seems as if all his freedom fighting, his struggles to help his people, and his growth as a political thinker and a consensus builder came together only during his years in prison. Most people grow weaker in jail. For Nelson Mandela, prison was the forge that strengthened his iron will.

Mandela had already been in jail for two years when his life sentence began. He was 46 years old. He left behind his wife, his children, his work, and settled in at Robben Island. It had changed for the worse since his last stay. Now it was home to many long-term prisoners, all divided by skin color. "You have no idea of the cruelty of man against man until

Today, the prison on Robben Island has been converted into a museum.

you have been in a South African prison with white warders and black prisoners," said Mandela.

The men rose at 5:30 in the morning. They cleaned their tiny, cold cells and washed in cold water from a pail. Breakfast was corn mush, with a drink of burned corn mixed with water to look like coffee.

Mandela's cell was tiny. When he lived in it, there was no bed, just a mat on the floor.

After that, they spent the morning in the wintry prison yard, hammering stones into gravel. No talking. For lunch, more mush. Then back to the rocks. At four, it was "bathtime," with seawater in buckets. Dinner: yet more mush, sometimes with a bit of carrot or cabbage or gristly meat. Sleep at eight—although the lights stayed on all day and night. The men slept on flat woven mats, in their clothes, with three prison-issued blankets thin enough to read through.

The men were not allowed to listen to the radio or read newspapers. Only one visitor was allowed every six months. Winnie, thin and troubled, was Nelson's first visitor. They spoke about family matters—no politics!—through a glass window, with five guards standing by. After only 30 minutes, one shouted, "Time up! Time up!"

For this photograph, some prisoners (including Mandela) were put to work sewing instead of breaking stones.

Nelson would not see Winnie again for two years. Only one letter per prisoner, no more than 500 words, was allowed in every six months; only one letter was allowed out. Both would be examined for political information, and anything suspicious was filed away, never to be seen again. Letters that did reach the prisoners were heavily censored, with whole sections cut or blacked out.

At first, the political prisoners expected to serve about ten years, no more. But soon Mandela realized that there was no end in sight. And the conditions were getting even worse. In January 1965, the men were taken to the quarry. There Mandela and the others

POLITICAL PRISONERS

When people are put in jail because the government thinks that their ideas and actions pose a threat, they are called political prisoners.

68

used picks and shovels to dig through the rock to the lime (a mineral used in building and farming). The sun glared off the white quarry walls, making the work unbearably hot and the light blindingly bright. Mandela's eyes were damaged forever.

The days were long and the conditions miserable. But Nelson Mandela was not alone. He had been sent to prison with many of his closest friends in the freedom struggle. Walter Sisulu, Ahmed Kathrada, Govan Mbeki, Raymond Mhlaba, all men Mandela had known for years, were convicted in the Rivonia trial and were serving their sentences with him. "We supported each other and gained strength from each other," wrote Mandela. "We would fight inside as we had fought outside."

In 1995, Mandela demonstrated how he broke rocks in the quarry for 12 years.

Besides the Rivonia men, there were prisoners from other political parties. If all political prisoners were together in one place, the government reasoned, it would be easier to keep an eye on them. But that policy led to an exchange of ideas between the men. For Mandela, it was a chance to form links and bonds with activists he could never have reached on the outside.

69

"We were a universe of thirty people," remembered one man. They could talk together here and there during the day, but they had almost no contact with the other prisoners and the outside world. In 1965, more political prisoners arrived. Mac Maharaj, a member of MK who specialized in sabotage, became a close Mandela ally. Laloo Chiba, once a tailor, had a useful skill: He could write extremely small letters, creating miniature documents perfect for hiding or smuggling out.

Mandela quickly became the leader, and new arrivals were sent to him. His leadership combined his political skills with his chiefly self-possession, and most prisoners, no matter how different their outlook when they arrived, could find common ground with him.

Even the guards and prison officials respected Mandela. He explained ANC policies to officials and guards, sometimes convincing them that what the group wanted was fair and reasonable. The men asked for permission to study in the evenings, and under pressure from the Red Cross, prison officials agreed. Soon most of the prisoners were studying: Mandela for his advanced law degree, others for the equivalent of a grade-school education. Getting the books

70

and other materials they needed was a challenge for the students; any book might be rejected or censored.

Maharaj urged one prisoner who was studying economics to ask for *The Economist.* Laughing, the others said he might as well ask for *Newsweek*—*The Economist* is a well-known British news magazine that would certainly have been banned. Maharaj insisted that the guards would judge the magazine only by its name. He was right. For a little while, before officials caught on, the men were able to keep up with world news.

Newspapers and anything that told what was happening in the world were more precious than food. Information was completely hidden from the prisoners. The officials wanted them to feel cut off, abandoned. When Mandela was caught with a paper, he was sentenced to three terrible days in solitary confinement.

The Red Cross

The Red Cross, an international group founded in Switzerland in 1863, was originally designed to assist people injured in war. Today it still serves that purpose, but it is best known for its work in disaster relief. The group also acts as a human-rights watchdog in special situations, including monitoring the treatment of political prisoners.

Mandela and Sisulu agreed to this one photograph—the only clear picture of them from Robben Island—hoping it would help their cause. It was barely noticed at the time.

71

ASSASSIN

An assassin is a person who murders a political figure.

Loneliness and isolation were hard on all the men. So they devised ways to communicate. Kathrada and Maharaj collected empty matchboxes discarded by guards as they walked men to the quarry. Chiba wrote secret messages in tiny letters, then placed each in a matchbox and covered it with a false bottom. If the matchbox were opened by a guard, he would see only a plain piece of cardboard. But a prisoner would know to pry up the bottom and find the message beneath. The matchboxes, dropped in carefully chosen places, helped the political prisoners communicate with the general prisoners. But there were problems. "We could easily be foiled by something as simple as the rain," said Mandela. "We soon evolved more efficient methods."

They hid messages, wrapped in plastic, at the bottom of the barrel of corn mush leaving the kitchen, or under dirty dishes going back. Men in solitary confinement

In Pretoria, Mandela's labor was sewing dirty mailbags. At Robben Island, he and the other men worked in the quarries.

72

hid wrapped messages under the rim of the toilet, to be retrieved by the next prisoner. Prisoners wrote invisible messages in milk (donated by a prisoner with an ulcer), then revealed them with disinfectant. Often Chiba wrote his tiny script on toilet paper, but the authorities found some of those messages and started limiting toilet paper to eight squares per prisoner per day.

Communicating with the outside world was even more difficult and dangerous. Visitors were searched. Only lawyers met prisoners privately and avoided the searches. But the rooms where they met were bugged.

Meanwhile, in the outside world, things were changing quickly. Verwoerd was killed by a Coloured assassin, and prison officials cracked down on Robben Island, as if they thought the men there were part of a plot. Suddenly the men were not allowed to talk while working in the quarry— the only thing that had made the work bearable. One guard was especially brutal, urinating beside the men as they ate and constantly making up serious charges that would lead to solitary confinement.

Conditions were at their worst when Helen Suzman, one of the few liberal members of parliament, visited and persuaded authorities to make improvements. The cruelest guards disappeared. The men were issued long pants instead of the shorts

PARLIAMENT

The South African and British Parliaments are similar to the U.S. Congress; they are the law-making branch of government.

73

that turned them into "boys." Warmer clothes were issued, and the food got a little better. The men were allowed to talk. And the senseless charges that sent prisoners into solitary slowed to a trickle.

"Time may seem to stand still for those of us in prison," wrote Mandela, "but it did not halt for those outside." His mother journeyed from Transkei to see him in early 1968. "My mother suddenly seemed very old," he said sadly. With her came Makgatho and Makaziwe, Nelson's son and daughter, now a grown man and woman. Where had the years gone?

Mandela was so happy to see them. But he was saddened by thoughts of his shortcomings as a son and a father. His mother had had a hard life, and Nelson had only been able to

Winnie Mandela, freed from prison after 17 months, holds a friend's baby—born on the day she was arrested.

help her for a few short years while he worked as a lawyer. His children had turned into adults without him. When Nelson's mother died just weeks after the visit, he felt even more strongly that he had failed her.

Time moved on for the rest of his family, too. In May 1969, Winnie was charged with reviving the ANC and arrested; the girls, ten-year-old Zeni and eight-year-old Zindzi, were torn away from her skirts. She went into solitary confinement in Pretoria Prison—no bail, no visitors—where she was questioned constantly. There she stayed for 17 months. Meanwhile, her husband was tormented with worry: "What were the authorities doing to my wife? How would she bear up? Who was looking after our daughters?"

More bad news came in July 1969, in a short telegram from Mandela's son Makgatho. Thembi, Nelson's oldest son, had died in a car accident. "What can one say about such a tragedy?" Mandela wrote long after, still without words to describe his pain.

He went to his cell and lay down. He remembered Thembi as a little boy, wearing a huge jacket that had belonged to Nelson, the father he so rarely saw. When Nelson left, Thembi had stood up tall and said, "I will look after the family while you are gone."

Hours passed. Eventually Walter Sisulu came. He read the telegram, then sat by his friend on the floor, holding his hand as another day slipped into night.

chapter 10

The University

Nelson Mandela spent so much time in jail that his experience can be looked at not a month at a time or a year at a time, but a decade at a time.

The 1960s were the worst. The political prisoners were sentenced to hard labor, day after day. The food was almost inedible, the men could be sent to solitary at any time, visitors and news were almost nonexistent, and basic human rights were denied. But by the late 1960s, conditions had improved.

The men were required to attend a Sunday-morning religious service, led by a visiting preacher. Father Hughes slipped news into his sermons. Reverend Jones urged

The lights were always on at Robben Island. Even after they were freed, many of the men could never sleep in the dark again.

prisoners to reconcile themselves to the whites, until Mandela's friend Eddie Daniels called out, "We've been seeking reconciliation for the last 75 years!" Brother September was delighted when a prisoner offered to lead a prayer. He asked the worshipers to close their eyes and pray, and everyone did—except for Daniels, who tiptoed to the pulpit, opened the preacher's briefcase, quietly removed his London *Sunday Times,* and scurried back to his seat with it.

Antigone

Antigone, written by the Greek playwright Sophocles around 450 BC, tells the story of Antigone, a young woman who risks her own life in order to do what is right. Creon, the king of Thebes, has vowed to kill anyone who buries the body of the treasonous Polynices, Antigone's brother. Although she is betrothed to the king's son, Antigone defies the king by burying Polynices. At the heart of *Antigone* is a debate about the responsibilities of leadership: Does Creon owe his loyalty to his country, or to his own family?

Another distraction was the prison's drama society. At Fort Hare, Mandela had once played John Wilkes Booth, the assassin of Abraham Lincoln. Now he and the other men put on the ancient Greek play *Antigone,* with Mandela as Creon, the king who says that "obligations to the people take precedence over loyalty to an individual." It was a most fitting role for a man who had given up everything for his people.

As the 1970s began, Mandela continued to treat the prison guards with dignity. A guard even came to him with

77

Intelligence agencies

Many governments have a branch that gathers information about what enemies inside and outside the country are up to. How is this "intelligence" gathered? Through spying, by intercepting messages between suspicious people or groups, by breaking codes, even by analyzing newspaper articles. Some agencies go beyond simple news gathering to enforce their governments' policies. In the U.S., the CIA and other agencies are responsible for this work.

an escape plan: He would slip Mandela the key to the prison door, then drug the guards on duty that night. Mandela would go to a boat waiting on the beach, put on scuba gear, then swim eight miles (13 kilometers) underwater to Cape Town. He would be met by a waiting car and driven to the airport to flee the country.

Privately, Mandela and Sisulu agreed this plan would work only if James Bond were trying it. Mandela didn't encourage the guard, and eventually the man was transferred out. Years later, Mandela discovered that the escape had actually been created by South Africa's secret intelligence agency. If he had gone along with the plot, he would have been killed in a dramatic shoot-out at the airport.

Conditions at the prison were up and down. "An advancement might take years to win, and then be rescinded in a day," remembered Mandela. When a new commanding officer, Piet Badenhorst, was assigned to the prison, he honed in on Mandela as the source of problems. He hounded the troublemaker with crude comments and punishments. A reign of terror began, and the cruelty came to a head on

78

May 28, 1971. On that bitterly cold day, guards burst into the prison, ordered prisoners to strip down, and forced them to stand with their hands in the air. The men could hear the screams of other prisoners as they were tortured and beaten.

Finally Mandela was able to smuggle out a message pleading for help. Three judges arrived on the island to hear the prisoners' complaints. Mandela, chosen to represent the men, described the conditions under Badenhorst's command, including a beating that had taken place the night before.

"Be careful, Mandela," said Badenhorst. "If you talk about things you haven't seen, you will get yourself in trouble. You know what I mean."

Mandela turned to the judges. "Gentlemen . . . if he can threaten me here, in your presence, you can imagine what he does when you are not here." Within three months, Badenhorst was gone.

By this time, Robben Island was becoming known as "the University." Men were studying English, Afrikaans, art, geography, and math through correspondence courses, and those men taught what they learned to the others. "We became our own faculty, with our own professors, our own curriculum, our own courses," said Mandela.

> *"We became our own faculty, with our own professors, our own curriculum, our own courses."*
>
> –Nelson Mandela, in his autobiography

Even the history of the ANC was covered in a course.

Sisulu and Kathrada had an idea: Mandela should write his autobiography.

In 2004, Mandela finally got two of his old notebooks back. The prison official who had confiscated them made the presentation.

A simple plan—but hard to do. Mandela would write all night, sometimes disguising what he wrote as letters. Each day Kathrada and Sisulu reviewed ten pages. Chiba secretly copied the pages in tiny writing, "reducing ten pages of foolscap [large writing paper] to a single small sheet of paper," Mandela marveled. The originals were buried in three cocoa containers in the courtyard where no one would find them . . . until the spot was dug up to build a new wall. The friends managed to destroy two containers, but the third was discovered. As punishment, Mandela, Sisulu, and Kathrada were forbidden to study for four years.

The tiny copied pages survived, and were smuggled out by Maharaj when his sentence was up in 1976. Eventually, in 1994, they became part of Mandela's autobiography, *Long Walk to Freedom,* an international best seller.

While Mandela and the other political prisoners were struggling to be heard, Winnie was struggling to raise her

80

children and continue the fight for freedom. She became involved with South Africa's rising Black Consciousness movement, led by Steve Biko and inspired by pride in the black experience and the civil-rights victories in Africa and the United States. Biko was banned in 1973, but Black Consciousness became increasingly popular in South Africa.

Steve Biko died in police custody in 1977, setting off mass protests.

Black Consciousness

The Black Consciousness movement was based on the idea that pride in being black was the first step to freedom. "Black man, you are on your own," said the group's leader, Steve Biko—that is, blacks should not depend on whites to give them freedom; they should have the strength and determination to take it for themselves. Black Consciousness empowered many black South Africans to rise up against white rule.

BIKO AND SOLIDARITY

BLACK PEOPLE'S CONVENTION
TRIBUTE TO THE LATE
HONORARY PRESIDENT
BANTU STEPHEN BIKO
One Azania: One Nation

Then, on June 16, 1976, riots broke out in Soweto when students protested the government's ruling that half of all classes in high school had to be taught in Afrikaans, which many thought of as the language of the oppressor. Ten thousand blacks marched—and the police fired on them. Hector Pieterson, a 13-year-old boy, was killed, then two whites. The Soweto Uprising, led by Black Consciousness activists, became a battle that lasted until the next year and left over a thousand people dead.

Soon, arrested Black Consciousness leaders began to arrive on Robben Island, bringing news of the revolt. ANC leaders were excited to learn that the freedom movement was still alive. But the new prisoners were different. They argued. They punched guards. They didn't want to study.

During the Soweto uprising, rioters used cars to block roads.

Although Mandela appreciated some aspects of Black Consciousness, he felt that its focus on blackness was not in harmony with the important concepts of cooperation and inclusion. Slowly, this "old man" of the protest movement calmed the angry young prisoners. "How I changed!" said one later. "All because I met Nelson Mandela and learned from him. . . . I began to question some of my Black Consciousness beliefs, because here was our leader preaching unity and nonracialism."

Outside his own country, however, Mandela seemed largely forgotten. The U.S. stayed out of South African politics; in the 1970s, the government eased pressure on South Africa to end apartheid. The British government also chose to look away. In 1972, Oliver Tambo observed that, if the South African government had not been financially supported by the U.S. and the United Kingdom, it would "long ago have gone bankrupt even while we were fighting, literally, with

The U.S. attitude toward apartheid

For many years, the United States took a hands-off approach toward South African apartheid, partly because it saw the white government as a valuable ally against communism. However, in the 1980s, in response to widespread protests at home, the U.S. government started putting pressure on South Africa to end apartheid, and many private companies took back money they had invested in the South African economy—actions which played an important role in the eventual downfall of apartheid.

83

our bare hands." And as the government collapsed for lack of money, apartheid would have fallen, too.

On Robben Island, a shortage of guards meant the end of hard labor. Mandela was still under his four-year ban from formal study, but he was allowed to talk with other prisoners and write. He took the opportunity to read novels, although anything with any hint of political meaning was forbidden. (Communists are sometimes called Reds, so "a request for a book with the word red in the title, even if it was *Little Red Riding Hood,* would be rejected," he recalled.) Mandela also had a garden, and all the men played tennis; their court was the prison courtyard painted green, with a rigged-up net.

But Nelson saw Winnie only very rarely, and contact visits were not permitted; they still shouted to each other through a small glass window. Meanwhile, Winnie was being harassed by the government with threats and unfounded charges. After one six-month jail term, she altered Zindzi's birth certificate to make her 16 (the minimum age for prison visitors) rather than 15, then took her to meet the father she had not seen since

> *"It was a dizzying experience . . . to suddenly hug one's fully grown child."*
>
> –Nelson Mandela, in his autobiography

she was three. Nelson was both delighted and saddened to see his littlest girl, now almost a grown woman.

Soon after, Winnie was not just banned—she was banished, to a shack

in a small, remote village called Brandfort. She had "no heat, no toilet, no running water," Mandela was pained to discover. She was under constant police surveillance.

The family had a bright spot in the late 1970s, when Zeni married a prince of Swaziland. Mandela was not able to meet with the young man personally, so he asked his lawyer George Bizos to interview him.

Swaziland

The small country of Swaziland is almost completely surrounded by South Africa. But its history is very different. It was ruled by the British from about 1903 until 1968, when it became independent. In 1973, the king, Sobhuza II, rejected the country's British-style constitution and became an absolute monarch. Today his grandson, King Mswati III, is often criticized for living lavishly while ignoring the poverty of his people.

Bizos reported that the groom seemed like a fine young man and, after all, he was a prince. "I told George to tell the young man that he was getting a Thembu princess," said Mandela.

As part of the Swazi royal family, Zeni was allowed to visit Nelson in a regular room rather than the walled-off visiting room. She and her husband brought their new baby. "It was a truly wondrous moment," remembered Mandela. Zeni raced across the room, and her father embraced her. "It was a dizzying experience, as though time had sped forward in a science fiction novel, to suddenly hug one's fully grown child," Mandela said later. He held the baby, too, "soft in [his] rough hands," and helped choose a name for her: Zaziwe. It means "hope."

chapter 11

Free Mandela!

While playing tennis in 1979, Mandela felt a sharp pain in his heel. Recently, the prison administration had become very interested in his aches and pains, worried about what the world would think if his health suffered. When Mandela won the Nehru Award for International Understanding, Indian Prime Minister Indira Gandhi, Nehru's daughter, had said, "Wherever people care for freedom and human dignity, Nelson Mandela's name is known."

Two burly young guards took Mandela, in handcuffs, to see a Cape Town doctor. The sea was rough, and there was just one lifejacket. Mandela vowed to himself, "If this boat goes under, I will commit my last sin on this earth and run over those two boys to get that lifejacket."

Safely on the mainland for the first time in 15 years, Mandela had bone fragments removed from his heel. "The nurses fussed over me a good deal," wrote Mandela. And he learned something: "I sensed a thawing in the relationship between black and white. The doctor and nurses had treated me in a natural way as though they had been dealing with blacks on a basis of equality all their lives. This was something new and different."

Soon after his return to Robben Island, where the new pajamas and robe Mandela had received from the nurses

made him the envy of the other prisoners, the men made a breakthrough. They were allowed to get newspapers—heavily censored, but still, news.

One story that Mandela was not allowed to see appeared in the Johannesburg *Sunday Post* in 1980. "FREE MANDELA!" roared its headline. Readers could sign a mail-in petition asking for the release of Nelson Mandela. The story was part of a brilliant idea by Oliver Tambo and the ANC—a plan to remind people that Mandela was still in prison, still full of hope for his country. By making Mandela a household name, the ANC hoped to personalize the fight against apartheid. Despite Indira Gandhi's words, few people outside Africa knew who Nelson Mandela was. Many people who saw posters reading "FREE MANDELA!" thought Mandela's first name was Free.

Meanwhile, MK sabotaged power stations, police stations, a refinery, and a military base, alerting the

Pictures of Nelson Mandela gave a face to the anti-apartheid struggle.

government of the new prime minister, P. W. Botha, that the struggle was still alive. K. D. Matanzima, Mandela's nephew, seized power in Thembuland. Matanzima became a dictator, and the South African government supported him, partly because he allowed them to turn Transkei into a Bantustan, a government-approved "native area." Another government favorite was Mangosuthu Buthelezi, the head of the

P. W. Botha wanted to find a way out of South Africa's troubles.

Zulu Bantustan. In 1975, Buthelezi revived a Zulu activist group called Inkatha and presented himself as an African leader in the style of Shaka, the great Zulu warrior.

One day, the prison commander squeezed into Mandela's cell unexpectedly. "We are transferring you," he told him. Mandela was astounded. Where? Why?

No answers. But Sisulu, Mhlaba, and Andrew Mlangeni, another of the older ANC prisoners, were also being transferred, right now. "Everything that I had accumulated in nearly two decades could fit in [a] few boxes," Mandela wrote. Hustled out, they were soon on the boat to Cape Town's Pollsmoor Prison.

The four men, the only political prisoners at Pollsmoor, got their own prison "penthouse." Real "beds, with sheets, and towels, [were] a great luxury for men who had spent much of the past eighteen years sleeping on thin mats on a

88

stone floor," marveled Mandela. The food was actually good. They read newspapers and had a radio.

The men felt more isolated in the posh cell, however, than they had on the island. There, they had been able to talk with many other political prisoners. Now, suddenly, it was just the four of them—five when Kathrada joined them a few weeks later.

Family visits were more frequent. When Winnie came in 1984, the guard announced a special surprise—contact visits. "I kissed and held my wife for the first time in all these many years," said Mandela. "It was as if I were still dreaming."

It was a rare moment of joy in Mandela's family. Exiled in Brandfort, Winnie had grown reckless. She became friendly with dishonest activists and others who were not as selfless as her husband. The children, all adults now, had their own complex lives. Zeni settled down after her marriage, eventually having three children. Zindzi was a talented writer; her poetry book, *Black as I Am,* was praised by critics, but she had troubled relationships. Makgatho struggled in school, and stopped writing or visiting his father at all. Makaziwe, divorced in the late 1970s, felt her father did not value her.

At least Mandela felt closer to his family when he could see them more often. It was easier to feel connected to the outside world at Pollsmoor. But the news wasn't good. In 1981, an ANC office in Mozambique was raided by South African soldiers, and 13 ANC supporters were killed. Forty-two more died in a similar attack in nearby Lesotho. In retaliation, MK set off a car bomb in downtown Pretoria, killing 19 people and injuring more than 200. Then the South African government bombed the ANC's London office. Violence was escalating.

Botha, the prime minister, offered Mandela a deal. He would be freed if he "unconditionally rejected violence as a political instrument." But Mandela would not. He "felt a profound horror" that innocent people were being hurt. Yet he knew that violence would be a necessary tool in troubled South Africa as long as the government did not hesitate to use violence against the people. The situation was different in the U.S., a democracy where police and military violence against protesters always caused public outcry and where, in general, the nonviolent tactics of civil-rights leaders like Martin Luther King Jr. were successful.

Martin Luther King Jr.

Martin Luther King Jr., the great American civil-rights activist, used nonviolent tactics to fight racism in the United States. His message, vividly captured in his famous "I Have a Dream" speech, was always one of peace and harmony. He was assassinated in 1968, not long after saying, "I am not going to allow anybody to pull me so low as to use the very methods that perpetrated evil throughout our civilization . . . I'm sick and tired of violence."

South Africa was a police state, where the government often used violence to control the people.

Mandela refused to accept Botha's conditions. On February 10, 1985, before a packed stadium in Soweto, Mandela's daughter Zindzi read his response. It was the first time anyone in South Africa had heard his words legally for more than 20 years.

90

Zindzi Mandela was carried to the stage by supporters to deliver her father's message.

"I am not a violent man," wrote Mandela. "Let [Botha] renounce violence. Let him say that he will dismantle apartheid. . . . I cherish my own freedom dearly, but I care even more for your freedom. I cannot and will not give any undertaking at a time when I and you, the people, are not free." As Zindzi read the message, people wept with joy that Mandela still fought on, even after 22 years in jail.

"Your freedom and mine cannot be separated," her father wrote. "I will return."

Mandela's refusal of the government's offer was news in South Africa and around the world.

91

chapter 12

Retreat through a Silver Bridge

All through South Africa, violence continued. Necklacing—killing a victim by lighting a tire filled with gasoline around his neck—became a horrifying symbol of black-on-black violence in South Africa. Anarchy, revolution, and civil war were very close. And at last, around the world, banks and governments finally started sending the message that apartheid was unacceptable by investing less money in South Africa.

The only hope for peace and stability in South Africa would be releasing Mandela, to show that the government was willing to give blacks a voice. Though he presented an immovable front to the public, behind the scenes Botha told his minister of justice, Kobie Coetsee, "You know, we have painted ourselves in a corner. Can you get us out?" The government wanted to start negotiating with

Minister of Justice Kobie Coetsee led government talks with Mandela.

Mandela. With money pouring out of the country as foreign governments pulled investments in a quiet financial protest against apartheid, it was time to try and reach a settlement with Nelson Mandela, the greatest anti-apartheid leader.

Calm and resolute, Mandela continued his prison routine. There was nothing about him, wrote Kathrada, to give "the slightest hint that he is the man about whom there is such an upsurge of feeling throughout the world." Everyone was frightened, though, when a routine physical exam revealed that Mandela needed prostate surgery. Winnie flew to Cape Town—on the same plane, by coincidence, as Coetsee. After the flight took off, Winnie barged into first class and started talking to him. By the time the plane landed, he had agreed to meet Mandela in the hospital.

Supporting Mandela was dangerous in a country full of turmoil. Here, policemen use horsewhips to beat protesters.

Mandela welcomed Coetsee as if he were the host at a party. He saw that "the government, in its slow and tentative way, was reckoning that they had to come to some accommodation with the ANC. Coetsee's visit was an olive branch."

After the operation, Mandela was taken back to Pollsmoor—but not to his roommates on the top floor. He was presented with three large cells all to himself. He had more space . . . but he was alone, for the first time in 24 years.

The full weight of his country's troubles bore down on him. He realized that he alone had the power to help. He wanted to reach out to the government. Would the other ANC members agree? They would surely tell him no. "But I was confident that the enemy itself wanted a retreat, through a silver bridge," he wrote. The great consensus builder would have to stand alone.

He wrote to Coetsee, suggesting "talks about talks." Soon Coetsee brought a council of seven "eminent persons" to meet Mandela.

Black-on-black violence added to South Africa's many problems.

The prison tailor whipped up a
three-piece suit for the occasion, and
the group—which included General
Olusegun Obasanjo of Nigeria and
former Australian prime minister
Malcolm Fraser—was impressed
by Mandela's command of the
political situation. "There is
nothing like a long spell in prison
to focus your mind," he told them dryly.

Winnie Mandela was Nelson's
greatest support during his
prison years—but she could
be a loose cannon.

Winnie continued to be Nelson's
lifeline, bringing him news and keeping his spirits up.
"Mother of a Nation," she was sometimes called, and she was
an inspiration in many ways. But there was another side of
Winnie—confrontational, angry, foolish, even violent. She told
a crowd, "We have no guns—we have only stones, boxes of
matches, and petrol. Together, hand in hand, with our boxes of
matches and our necklaces we shall liberate this country."

Mandela was shocked. The situation could not get much
darker—a state of emergency had been declared by the
government, and now his own wife was encouraging savage
violence. "But often, the most discouraging times are precisely
the time to launch an initiative. At such times people are
searching for a way out of their dilemma," Mandela wrote.

He asked General W. H. Willemse, the commissioner of
prisons, to send a message to Coetsee: Nelson Mandela wished
to see him. A few minutes later, still dressed in his prison

clothing, Mandela was in the general's car, headed for Coetsee's home. It was an astounding development.

Mandela's struggles were finally attracting worldwide attention, even in London, where leaders had supported South Africa's government for so many years.

Coetsee greeted him at the door, and the men sat down and talked for three hours. "I was struck by his sophistication and willingness to listen," remembered Mandela. It was as if, after all the years of struggle and misunderstanding, all the problems of South Africa had come down to two men, one white, one black, talking.

At last Mandela, lost in thought, was driven through the night, back to his cell. A tiny step, a huge step. Mandela had taken the risk of angering the ANC. Coetsee had taken the risk of angering his government. But that secret meeting, so casual on the surface, was the beginning of the new South Africa.

Slowly, the government began preparing Mandela for release. On the day before Christmas in 1986, Colonel Gawie Marx, a prison official, stopped by his cell and asked, "Mandela, would you like to see the city?"

"Yes," said Mandela. The officer led him through 15 locked metal doors.

Imagine Nelson Mandela stepping through that last door into the sunlight. Everything was the same, yet everything was different. Even the waiting car was new to Mandela. The guard remembered that "He tried to open this door. He was looking for a button to press. That year when he got to prison, the cars didn't have handles which lift up. . . . He didn't know how to open it."

Later, Mandela would remember his trip to Cape Town with fondness: "It was absolutely riveting to watch the simple activities of people out in the world: old men sitting in the sun, women doing their shopping, people walking their dogs. . . . I felt like a curious tourist in a strange and remarkable world."

Marx stopped the car outside a shop. "Would you like a cold drink?" he asked. When he went inside, Mandela considered running. "For the first time in twenty-two years, I was out in the world and unguarded," he later wrote. But he realized that if he escaped, he would be sacrificing his country's freedom for his personal freedom. He stayed in the car.

That was the first of many outings—to the mountains, to the beach, to tea shops and farms. No one ever recognized Mandela. His most recent clear pictures had been taken in 1963.

In 1987, Coetsee formed a secret group to meet with Mandela: Coetsee himself; General Willemse; Fanie van der Merwe, the director general of the prisons department; and Niel Barnard, the head of the National Intelligence Service, South Africa's version of the CIA.

Mandela consulted with the other ANC leaders at last. Did they agree it was time to negotiate with the government? Sisulu did. Kathrada did not. Mhlaba asked, "What have you been waiting for?" But Tambo, his closest friend on the outside, sent a note saying he had heard that Mandela was talking to the government and hinting that his semi-solitary existence must have unhinged him.

The group met weekly. The first issue they discussed was violence. "If the oppressor uses violence, the oppressed have no alternative but to respond violently," Mandela told them. They also talked about the ANC's relationship with the Communist Party; the government was certain that the few white communists in the ANC were controlling the many blacks. Finally, exasperated, Mandela said, "Well, there are four of you and only one of me, and you cannot control me or get me to change my mind. What makes you think the Communists can succeed where you have failed?"

The next question: If the tables were turned, how would the majority treat the minorities? Mandela quoted the Freedom Charter: "South Africa belongs to all who live in it, black and white."

ARSON

Arson is setting a fire on purpose, to kill a person or to destroy property.

98

While the men talked, turmoil continued. On a visit, Winnie told Nelson that their old home in Orlando had been destroyed by arsonists. All the family's photos and papers had been lost in the fire. Even the slice of wedding cake that Winnie had carefully set aside for the day her husband was released from prison was gone.

Mandela was saddened, and he was sick, too, with a cough that would not go away. Doctors discovered that he had tuberculosis, probably encouraged by his damp cell. The government was in a flurry, realizing, according to London's *Sunday Times,* that "the only thing

Pictures from Mandela's Black Pimpernel days were used on posters and signs.

worse than a free Mandela is a dead Mandela." He stayed at the hospital for six weeks, charming the nurses; then he was transferred to a luxurious rehabilitation clinic, where he was the first black patient ever (and where the nurses were, of course, enchanted with him). Coetsee came to see him, accompanied by Major Marais, an officer assigned to watch over Mandela. While they talked, Mandela's breakfast arrived: eggs, buttered toast, and bacon. *Bacon!* Mandela had been on a low-cholesterol diet for years. As Mandela lifted his fork, Marais, who knew the doctors' orders, reached to take the tray away

99

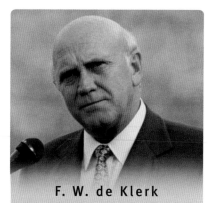

F. W. de Klerk

When he became president, F. W. de Klerk knew apartheid could not continue. The terrible violence and the international protests, combined with other pressures inside and outside the country, told him that it was time to end the oppressive policy. But he was probably also driven by his own sense of right and wrong. In 2005, he said he ended apartheid "to bring justice to everybody."

from him. Mandela held on tight and said, "Major, I am sorry. If this breakfast will kill me, then today I am prepared to die."

After his recovery, Mandela was moved again, this time to Victor Verster Prison. But instead of stopping at the prison gates, the car drove on, to a small cottage shaded by fir trees. Only the guards and the razor-wire-topped walls spoiled the pretty picture. "Even so, it was a lovely place and situation," said Mandela, "a halfway house between prison and freedom."

Mandela settled down in his new home, with a personal cook and his own guards. The secret meetings continued, the same discussions over and over. Then, in early 1989, P.W. Botha had a stroke. Years before, he had eliminated the title of prime minister. Now he refused to give up the title of president. Under these strange circumstances, F. W. de Klerk, a reliable party politician, was selected by the National Party as party leader. After a national

election in September 1989, de Klerk became president and
Botha was forced to step down.

Although his living situation was much improved and he
had gained the respect of the government, Mandela found he
had new problems. Troubled, impoverished Winnie, finally
released from her banishment, had used young Soweto gang
members as her bodyguards. The boys were wild and cruel, and
when one was murdered, Winnie was accused of involvement
in his killing. What really happened to Stompie Seipei may
never be known, but his murder and the ensuing trials and
accusations tarnished Nelson's reputation as well as Winnie's.

Still, Mandela was overjoyed in July 1989, when his entire
family gathered at his little house to celebrate his 71st birthday.
(For his 70th birthday, London had hosted Freedomfest,
a rock festival televised in sixty countries.) Never before had
Mandela had everyone together. He called the party a
"deep, deep pleasure."
But, he sighed, "The
only pain was the
knowledge that I
had missed such
occasions for so
many years."

Winnie always
dressed up to visit
Nelson in prison.
For this trip, she brought
Zindzi and some of the
grandchildren.

Desmond Tutu

Desmond Tutu, born in 1931, became involved in South Africa's politics as chaplain of Fort Hare in the early 1960s. He urged reconciliation as a solution to apartheid. Eventually he rose in the Anglican church to become archbishop of Cape Town, and he was awarded the Nobel Peace Prize in 1984 for his work "as a unifying leader figure in the campaign to resolve the problem of apartheid." In the 1990s, he led the Truth and Reconciliation Commission.

Shortly before this, Mandela had been smuggled in to meet Botha, still serving as president. Before the visit, Willemse politely asked Mandela's blood type . . . just in case. Botha and Mandela discussed history and culture, not issues. The meeting was pleasant, and Mandela felt progress had been made. But then Botha resigned, and de Klerk was sworn in as president.

De Klerk was not known as a reformer, and yet he allowed a rally protesting police brutality, led by Archbishop Desmond Tutu. "A new and different hand was on the tiller," Mandela noted.

It certainly was. In October 1989, seven of Mandela's fellow Robben Island prisoners were released without conditions, including Sisulu, Mhlaba, Kathrada, and Mlangeni. (Govan Mbeki, older than the other men, had been released earlier.) The men were even permitted to speak publicly about the ANC.

Practical de Klerk was probably driven by economic pressures rather than a sense of fairness, but in the end the results were what Mandela and the ANC had dreamed of: the beginning of the end of apartheid. Beaches were opened to blacks and whites alike. Segregation on buses and at parks, theaters, restaurants, libraries, and bathrooms ended. But would de Klerk's moves mean true equality? Mandela and his former fellow prisoners met with the new president in December 1989, outlining their concerns.

De Klerk listened. And on February 2, 1990, he went to the South African Parliament and began to lay the groundwork for a democratic South Africa. The bans were lifted on the ANC and more than 30 other political organizations. Political prisoners were freed. The death penalty was suspended. "The time for negotiation has arrived," announced de Klerk.

"Our world had changed overnight," wrote Mandela. Sadly, Oliver Tambo, exiled for so long, could not fully join in the rejoicing; he had had a stroke. But Mandela and the other old friends

Walter Sisulu, with his wife Albertina, celebrates his release from prison.

> "I felt—even at the age of seventy-one— that my life was beginning anew."
>
> –Nelson Mandela, in his autobiography

were both stunned and overjoyed. After all the years of struggle, apartheid had been swept away in a day.

A week later, de Klerk summoned Mandela to his office and, smiling, told him that he would be freed the very next day, February 11, 1990.

Nelson Mandela had spent 27 years in prison.

He awoke at 4:30 the next morning, after staying up late working on his speech. Winnie, Sisulu, and other supporters flew in on a hastily chartered flight. Mandela's prison house was a scene of commotion, packed with people. Just before four that afternoon, wearing a hastily tailored new suit, he and Winnie walked toward the prison gates.

The gates swung open, and Mandela saw hundreds of photographers and news cameras, in front of thousands of well-wishers of every color. The cameras "sounded like some great herd of metallic

In South Africa and around the world, Mandela's supporters rejoiced at the announcement that he would finally be released from prison.

beasts," recalled Mandela. Helicopters chopped overhead. Reporters shouted; everyone screamed and waved ANC flags. Mandela was both delighted and disoriented. Still, he said, "I felt—even at the age of seventy-one—that my life was beginning anew."

In the middle of the crowd, as he was pushed and pulled to a waiting car, Mandela raised his fist high above his head, in the sign of black power and pride. The crowd roared. It had been a long walk, but their leader was back.

The long walk had ended. Another was just beginning.

chapter **13**

Free at Last

South Africa couldn't be fixed overnight. Mandela held his first press conference at Archbishop Tutu's residence in Cape Town, then flew to Johannesburg to speak to a rally of 100,000 people. He spoke of the need for forgiveness, for education, for the end of violence. The crowd was spellbound.

Mandela settled briefly in Soweto with Winnie, living quietly—except for an unending stream of visitors, including old friends, journalists, and dignitaries. Then he set off on a world tour, during which he gathered support for the ANC and asked world leaders to continue sanctions against the South African government until negotiations were finished.

Winnie (left) and Oliver Tambo's wife, Adelaide, traveled with Mandela to London, but he was the star.

He traveled first within Africa: to Zambia, Zimbabwe, Namibia, and Algeria. In Sweden he saw Oliver Tambo, who was slowly recovering from his stroke. Everywhere he went, Mandela told people that he was just part of a greater whole: the African National Congress.

Mandela was greeted with joy wherever he went, from Africa to Europe to New York's Harlem, above.

New York gave Mandela parade, and lit the Empire State Building in ANC colors. He met with England's prime minister, Margaret Thatcher, and was introduced to Graça Machel, widow of the former president, in Mozambique. In India, he drank from the sacred Ganges River. He traveled to Indonesia, Australia, Japan—a celebrated guest worldwide.

Everywhere Mandela was treated as a hero, but he took the acclaim with modesty. He loved to tell about the little girl who asked him why he had spent so much time in jail. When he explained, she said, "You must be a very stupid old man."

The world adored him, but his own people were realizing that he did not have magical powers. Police attacked ANC demonstrators on March 26, 1990, and killed 12. Mandela told de Klerk that the government could not "talk about negotiations on the one hand and murder our people on the other." Clearly part of the government wanted to divide blacks to keep them from fighting as one united front.

Talks began in May 1990. The two groups of negotiators looked like soccer teams from different planets: The government had gathered 11 white, male Afrikaners, while the ANC had seven blacks, two whites, one Indian, and one Coloured, including two women. After weeks of discussions, Mandela made an historic offer: an immediate cease fire.

Meanwhile, he worked behind the scenes to rejoin the fragments of the ANC. Mandela, Sisulu, Tambo, and other older members of the group still dominated the decision making, but when new elections were held, Cyril Ramaphosa, head of the Mineworkers' Union, became president of the group.

Although he was negotiating with some of the most challenging personalities on earth, Mandela was determined to see the best in everyone. He truly wanted all people to have equal money, power, and human dignity.

South Africa seemed like it should be improving, but violence continued. In the rural Zulu area, KwaZulu-Natal, Inkatha had effectively declared war on ANC supporters, partly because Inkatha disagreed with the ANC's vision of a unified South Africa. This conflict killed more than 3,500 people between 1990 and 1993. Mandela tried to work with the difficult, angry Inkatha leader, Buthelezi. He made a speech to about 100,000 Zulus, begging them to "Take your guns, your knives, and your *pangas* [machetes], and throw them into the sea!" But his pleas fell on deaf ears. Mandela didn't know— although he suspected—that the government was secretly supporting Inkatha, encouraging the violence.

Why? To undermine Mandela and the ANC. The ongoing violence among blacks made whites believe the ANC was not capable of running the country—after all, they couldn't even control their own people. And by secretly supporting Inkatha, the white government was also dividing the black organizations.

At last, in July 1991, newspapers broke the story that the police had been funding Inkatha. "POLICE PAID INKATHA TO BLOCK ANC," blared the headlines. Top government officials lost their jobs, and de Klerk looked worst of all. A peace accord was reached between Mandela, de Klerk, and Buthelezi, but tensions continued.

Chief Mangosuthu Buthelezi (right) called for an end to black-on-black violence at a Zulu rally in 1991.

So being released from prison didn't mean the end of Nelson Mandela's problems. His country was still torn by violence, with more people being killed than ever before. And at home, his marriage to Winnie was unraveling.

As Winnie had stood by him, Nelson stood by her during her kidnapping trial.

Winnie and Nelson had been married for only four years before he went to prison. Now he had emerged at last, a much different man than Winnie remembered. She had stood by him during all the years he was away, had cared for their children, had struggled to continue the fight. Now the reality of having him home was difficult for her.

In 1991, Winnie's four-month-long trial for the kidnapping and assault of Stompie Seipei strained the marriage to the breaking point, and her wild behavior continued to distress and embarrass Nelson. Finally, in April 1993, with Tambo and Sisulu by his side, he announced to the public that he was separating from his wife. "Ladies and gentlemen, I hope you appreciate the pain I have gone through," he said.

Meanwhile, the freedom struggle was intensifying again. At the Convention for a Democratic South Africa, de Klerk and Mandela butted heads. Though both agreed that negotiations must continue, the ANC and the government could not come to terms. The ANC and its allies were to begin strikes, demonstrations, and boycotts—but then Inkatha raided a small township loyal to the ANC and killed 46 people, mostly women and children, in the group's fourth mass killing in a week. "My patience snapped," said Mandela. The government was making it easy for black citizens to be ruthlessly murdered. The ANC would not negotiate further.

More than four million workers stayed home on August 3 and 4, 1993. Protests were held in Pretoria, then in Bisho on September 7. As demonstrators marched, troops opened fire and killed 29 people. This time the government blinked. They agreed at least to accept a new elected assembly, which would create a new South African constitution. Partly because of this agreement, Mandela and de Klerk shared the Nobel Peace Prize for that year.

Soon after this triumph, however, Mandela suffered a terrible loss. Oliver Tambo died from a second stroke. "He had been snatched away from me just as we had finally been reunited," Mandela wrote mournfully. Tambo would have wanted to see the next step in South Africa: The date for the first democratic elections in the history of the country was set for April 27, 1994. One person, one vote—whether that person was white, Coloured, Indian, or black.

In South Africa, votes are cast for parties rather than individuals; the winning party then selects its president. The major parties would be de Klerk's National Party and, for the first time in history, the ANC, led by Nelson Mandela.

Campaigning in South Africa was more challenging than it is in the U.S., where the right to vote is well established. More than 20 million people, many unable to read or write, some frightened of any official place, would be voting for the first time. The ANC trained more than 100,000 people to help with voter education.

Their slogan was "A Better Life for All," and in public gatherings called People's Forums, Mandela explained how the ANC would help build the country's future by creating jobs, building housing, and offering health care and education. He enjoyed the forums; they reminded him of the public meetings he had witnessed at the Great Place in Thembuland 70 years before.

In South Africa's first democratic elections, the lines of voters were often miles long.

On the two days of the elections, the ANC's work paid off. People lined up before dawn, sometimes waiting five hours for their chance to vote. "After nearly three hundred and fifty years, three hundred and fifty minutes is nothing," one said.

The Nobel Prizes

The Nobel Prizes, created by Alfred Nobel, inventor of dynamite, have been given every year since 1901. They are awarded for outstanding achievement in physics, chemistry, medicine, literature, and peace. The peace prize is given to those who have made significant strides toward creating unity in our world. Winners are chosen by an international committee, and have included Martin Luther King Jr., Elie Wiesel, and Mother Teresa.

Mandela himself was one of the new voters. Setting out for the polling station on the second day of elections, he thought of all the freedom fighters who were no longer with him: Tambo, Luthuli, so many more who had stood side by side with him. "I did not go into that voting station alone," he said. "I was casting my vote with all of them." He marked an X in the ANC box, then "slipped my folded ballot paper into a simple wooden box. I had cast the first vote of my life."

When the votes were counted, the voice of the people was clear. The ANC won 62.6 percent of the vote. South Africa had a new president: Nelson Mandela.

113

chapter 14

President Mandela

President Mandela's first order of business was selecting a deputy, a position much like that of the U.S. vice president. The election agreement had specified that the new government would be a coalition, including members of the opposing parties. So de Klerk, as the leader of the National Party, would be one of the deputy presidents. Mandela chose Thabo Mbeki, the son of Robben Island prisoner Govan Mbeki and a respected ANC leader, as the other. Mbeki stood beside Mandela on May 10 as he was sworn in as the first black president of South Africa.

A billion people around the world watched the historic moment. The ceremony took place in Pretoria, before 4,000 guests. "Today, all of us do, by our presence here . . . confer glory and hope to newborn liberty," Mandela said in his speech. "Never, never, and never again shall it be that this beautiful land will again experience the oppression of one by another."

But the reality of running a country was hard. "We were taken from the bush, or from underground outside the country, or from prisons, to come and take charge," Mandela said later.

He won many over with his charisma. He would read prepared speeches, then take off his glasses and tell the press, "That's what my bosses said." Then he would tell a story from his own experience, about being criticized as a child or being spotted walking down a street. Still regal at 76 years old, yet homespun and wise, Mandela was a great father figure.

In cabinet meetings, where leaders from the opposing parties sat side by side, Mandela listened to all the opinions and then drew his own conclusions. Like Jongintaba, his boyhood mentor, "He took it like a chief," said Mac Maharaj. "He listened impassively, took everything in, and then intervened." Mandela continued to be the great consensus builder—only now he was not only reconciling individuals, but entire political parties and countries.

In 1996, a new constitution was ratified. Mandela acknowledged the different groups that had worked together to create it, saying, "Our consensus speaks of the maturing of our young democracy. It speaks of the trust that has grown in the blast furnace of practical work, as we, together, rolled up our sleeves to tackle the real problems."

President Nelson Mandela signed his country's new nonracial constitution on December 10, 1996.

Everyone, including Winnie Mandela, was invited to appear before the Truth and Reconciliation Commission.

In his presidency, Mandela was perhaps best known for his forgiveness. He called on old enemies and old friends alike, he visited Afrikaners and made them feel welcome in the new order, he embraced the press—at times he seemed almost too good to be true. But that was Mandela's nature: upbeat, positive, and optimistic. It had helped him through all the challenges of his life, and now it was helping him still.

It was important for his country to forgive without forgetting, Mandela thought, and in 1996 he helped launch the Truth and Reconciliation Commission (TRC). This group would collect the stories of all who had lived through apartheid, granting amnesty to those who had committed crimes in exchange for giving true testimony of the horrors of those years.

Many were unhappy with this plan—it let murderers, terrorists, and other criminals walk—but the TRC was able to gather fuller and more truthful accounts of events than any other group. Brilliant and humane, the

AMNESTY

Amnesty is the act of releasing a large group of people from punishment for their crimes.

116

TRC needed the full support of Nelson Mandela to gather the stories of a nation. Its motto was "I invite you to join in the search for truth, without which there can be no genuine reconciliation."

Horrifying stories emerged from this search for truth: Torture and killings were described in detail; dark secrets about the government—and the ANC—were revealed. Witnesses confessed how bodies had been burned to ashes or cut into unidentifiable pieces. The men who had killed the Black Consciousness leader Steve Biko described his death. The revelations were like reliving a nightmare, and yet they allowed the country to begin to heal.

"We must regard the healing of the South African nation as a process, not an event," said Mandela. The TRC, he said, had "helped us to move away from the past to concentrate on the present and the future."

Desmond Tutu presents the findings of the TRC to President Mandela.

The TRC was the greatest achievement of Mandela's five-year presidency. In 1996, de Klerk, whose relationship with Mandela had become tense, withdrew National Party members from the coalition government. ANC members took their places. Thabo Mbeki stayed, now the sole deputy president.

Before the fiftieth conference of the ANC, Mandela announced he would be stepping down as president of the group. Mbeki would take his place. The ANC celebrated their leader with giant signs that said "ALL POWER TO THE PEOPLE" and hundreds of yellow flowers. They had come a long way since Mandela's first conference so many years before.

In his closing remarks, Mandela spoke with emotion. "I look forward to that period when I will be able to wake up with the sun, to walk the hills and valleys of my country village, Qunu, in peace and tranquility." Nelson Mandela's long walk to freedom was coming to its end. But the road had a few more twists and turns ahead.

Mandela found happiness with Graça Machel.

Privately, he had been very lonely. When he saw Graça Machel, two years after their first meeting in 1990, he recognized another lonely person. Machel's husband had been killed in a suspicious 1986 airplane accident. Graça wore mourning black for several years. Active in political causes and beloved in her country, she was 27 years younger than Mandela. Still, their friendship deepened into love.

They were married, to set a "proper example for the young people," on Nelson Mandela's 80th birthday, July 18, 1998. The next day, the new couple danced at a huge party before jetting off for their honeymoon. The marriage was a truly happy ending. "The world needs symbols, probably nowadays more than before," said Graça about Mandela. "Whatever happens to him, it is a mark of the liberation of the African people."

In 1999, before he left the presidency, Mandela took a whirlwind world tour, saying good-bye to other world leaders. President Bill Clinton, a close friend, paid tribute by saying, "In every gnarly, knotted, distorted situation in the world where people are kept from becoming the best they can be, there is an apartheid of the heart. And if we really honor this stunning sacrifice of twenty-seven years, if we really rejoice in the infinite justice of this man happily married in the autumn of his life, if we really are seeking some driven wisdom from the power of his example, it will be to do whatever we can, however we can, wherever we can, to take the apartheid out of our own and others' hearts."

119

Epilogue

Nelson Mandela's last day as president of South Africa was June 16, 1999. He retired to a modest home in Qunu with his new wife. There he continues to work for a better world, sometimes acting as a negotiator in serious world crises. He is active with the struggle against HIV—his son Makgatho died of the disease in 2005—and tuberculosis, and, with Graça Machel, he works tirelessly for children's causes.

What is Nelson Mandela's legacy to his country? Many people think only of his forgiveness. But his work and his sacrifices laid the building blocks for a democratic South Africa. When this book was written in 2006, Mandela was still alive, still very active in the politics of his country and the world. Unlike many of the other figures who are featured in biographies, Nelson Mandela is recent history. He was freed from prison in 1991. He became president in 1994. Maybe you were born in 1994, or not too long after that. Your parents were probably grown-ups when Nelson Mandela was in office.

Walter Sisulu died in 2003. Like Mandela, he lived a long life—long enough to see real change happening in his country, and to have hope that democracy would live forever in South Africa. Perhaps Mandela's greatest gift was that he served his five-year presidency, working with

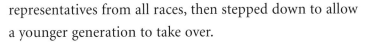

representatives from all races, then stepped down to allow a younger generation to take over.

Because he was so beloved, he could have taken over the presidency permanently and kept South Africa as his own personal kingdom. But Mandela truly believed in democracy and fair play. He truly believed in equality for the races. He truly believed that, in the end, good must triumph over racism, intolerance, and injustice. And he made that triumph happen.

Mandela named his HIV-awareness campaign after his former prisoner number.

Events in the Life of Nelson Mandela

July 18, 1918
Nelson Rolihlahla
Mandela is born in the
Transkei countryside.

1942
In Johannesburg, Mandela
begins his law work and
meets Walter Sisulu.

1944
Mandela marries
Evelyn Mase and joins
the ANC, forming the
Youth League.

1958
Mandela
marries
Winnie
Madikizela.

1962
Mandela travels
outside South Africa
to gain support
for the ANC. When
he gets back, he
is arrested and
sentenced to five
years in prison.

1930
Nelson's father dies;
Chief Jongintaba
takes charge of the
boy's upbringing.

1961
Mandela goes
underground to
form Umkhonto
we Sizwe (MK).

1956
The police arrest
Mandela for treason.
The Treason Trial
begins the next year.

1940
Mandela is expelled
from Fort Hare. While
studying there, he had
met Oliver Tambo.

1963
Lilliesleaf Farm at
Rivonia is raided.
Mandela and
others, charged
with sabotage, are
sentenced to life
imprisonment on
Robben Island.

1952
Mandela organizes the
Defiance Campaign
with other young ANC
leaders. Mandela
and Tambo opens for
business.

122

1980
Mandela is awarded the Nehru Award for International Understanding. The Free Mandela campaign gathers support.

1985
After an operation, Mandela is given a private cell at Pollsmoor.

December 1993
Mandela and F. W. de Klerk share the Nobel Peace Prize.

1988
As economic sanctions on South Africa tighten, Mandela is moved to a house at Victor Verster Prison.

April 27, 1994
Mandela votes for the first time—and is elected as South Africa's first black president.

1983
Mandela refuses Botha's offer of freedom. He will not reject violence unconditionally.

July 18, 1998
Mandela marries Graça Machel.

February 11, 1990
Mandela is released from prison. He served 27 years of his sentence.

1982
Mandela and others are moved to Pollsmoor Prison.

June 16, 1999
Mandela retires from the presidency. He remains active in many causes, including the fight against HIV/AIDS.

123

Bibliography

Lauré, Jason, and Ettagale Lauré. *South Africa: Coming of Age Under Apartheid*. New York: Farrar, Straus, Giroux, 1980.

Lewis, Anthony. "Uneasy Allies." *The New York Times Book Review,* February 6, 2006.

Maltz, Leora, ed. *Nelson Mandela*. San Diego: Greenhaven, 2004.

Mandela, Nelson. *Long Walk to Freedom: The Autobiography of Nelson Mandela*. Boston: Little, Brown and Company, 1994.

Mandela, Nelson. *Mandela: An Illustrated Autobiography*. Boston: Little, Brown and Company, 1996.

Mandela, Nelson and Richard W. Kelso (abridgment and connecting notes). *Long Walk to Freedom: The Autobiography of Nelson Mandela with Connections*. Austin, Texas: Holt, Rinehart and Winston, 1995.

McKee, Tim and Anne Blackshaw (photographs). *No More Strangers Now: Young Voices from a New South Africa*. New York: DK Ink, 1998.

Sampson, Anthony. *Mandela: The Authorized Biography*. New York: Knopf, 1999.

Schadeberg, Jürgen (compilation and photography). *Voices from Robben Island*. Braamfontein, South Africa: Ravan, 1994.

Thompson, Leonard. *A History of South Africa,* 3rd ed. New Haven: Yale University Press, 2001.

Welsh, Frank. *South Africa: A Narrative History*. New York: Kodansha, 1999.

Works Cited

(*LWTF = Long Walk to Freedom; MTAB = Mandela: The Authorized Biography*)
p. 7 "My father possessed…" *LWTF*, 6; p. 11 "I must have been a comical sight…" *LWTF*, 12; p. 13 "If one or two animals stray…" *LWTF*, 11-12 ; p. 14 "We have [promised you] manhood…" *LWTF*, 26; p. 14 "He had planted a seed…" *LWTF*, 26; p. 14 "Most of my classmates could outrun me…" *LWTF*, 29; p. 15 "We cannot allow these foreigners…" *LWTF*, 36; p. 15 "I had many new and sometimes conflicting ideas…" *LWTF*, 36; p. 17 "I would be dishonest if I said that the girl was…" *LWTF*, 47; p. 19 "I marked him at once as a man with great qualities…" *MTAB*, 33; p. 20 "in honor of your arrival" *LWTF*, 63; p. 21 "I cannot pinpoint a moment when I became politicized…" *LWTF*, 83; p. 22 "The better class of Native," *MTAB*, 36; p. 23 "If I could have done my work…" *MTAB*, 37; p. 24 "were prepared to treat Africans as human beings and their equals…" *MTAB*, 43; p. 29 "From the moment of the Nationalists' election…" *LWTF*, 97-98; p. 29 "Both nationalisms laid claim to the same piece of earth…" *MTAB*, 53; p. 30 "There are two bulls…" *MTAB*, 63; p. 31 "That day was a turning point in my life…" *MTAB*, 63; p. 37 "uppity" *MTAB*, 79; p. 39 "There are our enemies!" *MTAB*, 83; p. 39 "We have to employ new methods in our struggle…." *MTAB*, 86; p. 40 "tens of thousands of scraps of paper [that] came flooding in…" *MTAB*, 91; p. 44 "You are playing with fire…." *LWTF*, 173; p. 44 "bound together by love of [their] history…" *LWTF*, 176; p. 47 "Do you understand English?" *LWTF*, 184; p. 48 "I cannot say for certain if there is such a thing as love at first sight…" *LWTF*, 186; p. 49 "My sisters literally cried…" *MTAB*, 111; p. 49 "If your man is a wizard…" *LWTF*, 188; p. 49 "I don't think we need to be taught how to speak…." *MTAB*, 113; p. 49 "I've married trouble!" *MTAB*, 113; p. 50 "In every city, town, and village…" *MTAB*, 129; p. 53 "Africans must feel, act, and speak in one voice." *MTAB*, 141; p. 55 "The seconds I spent waiting for the light to change…" *LWTF*, 233; p. 55 "If the government reaction is to crush by naked force…." *LWTF*, 236; p. 56 "*Sebatana ha se bokwe ka diatla*…" *LWTF*, 236; p. 56 "what was least violent to individuals…" *LWTF*, 239; p. 56 "Only through hardship…" *LWTF*, 240-241; p. 57 "Amasi…what is it doing there?" *LWTF*, 242; p. 58 "We will resort to them over and over again." *MTAB*, 162; p. 59 "Why go back?" *MTAB*, 167; p. 59 "I was the symbol of justice in the court of the oppressor…" *MTAB*, 171; p. 60 "literally carrying on my back the history, culture, and heritage of my people." *LWTF*, 283; p. 60 "There is no end and no beginning…" *LWTF*, 363; p. 61 "*Dis die Eiland!*" *LWTF*, 297; p. 62 "Nelson, come here." *LWTF*, 299; p. 63 "Amandla!" *MTAB*, 185; p. 63 "It is not I, but the government…" *MTAB*, 187;

p. 63 "Was there any hope…" *MTAB*, 187; p. 64 "During my lifetime, I have dedicated myself…" *LWTF*, 322; p. 65 "I meant everything I said." *MTAB*, 195; p. 66 "You have no idea of the cruelty of man against man…" *MTAB*, 203; p. 68 "Time up! Time up!" *LWTF*, 352; p. 69 "We supported each other and gained strength from each other." *LWTF*, 341; p. 70 "We were a universe of thirty people." *MTAB*, 206; p. 72 "We could easily be foiled by something as simple as the rain." *LWTF*, 367; p. 74 "Time may seem to stand still for those of us in prison.…" *LWTF*, 387; p. 75 "What were the authorities doing to my wife?" *LWTF*, 389; p. 75 "What can one say about such a tragedy?" *LWTF*, 389; p. 75 "I will look after the family while you are gone." *LWTF*, 390; p. 77 "We've been seeking reconciliation for the last 75 years!" *LWTF*, 394; p. 79 "Be careful, Mandela.…" *LWTF*, 402; p. 79 "We became our own faculty…" *LWTF*, 406-407; p. 80 "reducing ten pages of foolscap…" *LWTF*, 415; p. 81 "Black man, you are on your own." From the Web site www.sahistory.org.za; p. 83 "How I changed!" *MTAB*, 274; p. 84 "A request for a book with the word 'red' in the title…" *LWTF*, 428; p. 84 "It was a dizzying experience…" *LWTF*, 431; p. 85 "no heat, no toilet, no running water…" *LWTF*, 429; p. 85 "I told George to tell the young man…" *LWTF*, 430; p. 86 "Wherever people care for freedom…" From the Web site www.anc.org.za; p. 86 "If this boat goes under…" *LWTF*, 438; p. 86 "The nurses fussed over me a great deal…" *LWTF*, 439; p. 88 "We are transferring you." *LWTF*, 443; p. 88 "beds, with sheets, and towels…" *LWTF*, 447; p. 89 "I kissed and held my wife…" *LWTF*, 450-451; p. 90 "unconditionally rejected violence…" *LWTF*, 454; p. 90 "I am not going to allow anybody to pull me so low…" "Uneasy Allies," *The New York Times Book Review*, February 6, 2006, page 9.; p. 91 "I am not a violent man.…" *LWTF*, 455; p. 92 "You know, we have painted ourselves in a corner…" *MTAB*, 331; p. 93 "the slightest hint that he is the man…" *MTAB*, 337-338; p. 94 "the government, in its slow and tentative way, was reckoning…" *LWTF*, 456; p. 94 "But I was confident that the enemy itself wanted a retreat…" *MTAB*, 341; p. 94 "talks about talks." *LWTF*, 459; p. 95 "There is nothing like a long spell in prison to focus your mind." *MTAB*, 343; p. 95 "We have no guns…" *MTAB*, 344; p. 95 "But often, the most discouraging times…" *LWTF*, 461; p. 96 "I was struck by his sophistication…" *LWTF*, 462; p. 97 "Mandela, would you like to see the city?" *LWTF*, 463; p. 97 "He tried to open this door…" From an interview with Christo Brand on the Web site www.pbs.org/wgbh/pages/frontline/shows/Mandela; p. 97 "It was absolutely riveting to watch the simple activities of people out in the world…" *LWTF*, 463; p. 97 "Would you like a cold drink?" *LWTF*, 463; p. 97 "For the first time in twenty-two years…" *LWTF*, 463; p. 98 "What have you been waiting for?" *LWTF*, 466; p. 98 "If the oppressor uses violence…" *LWTF*, 468; p. 98 "Well, there are four of you…" *LWTF*, 469; p. 98 "South Africa belongs to all who live in it…" *LWTF*, 469; p. 99 "the only thing worse than a free Mandela is a dead Mandela." *MTAB*, 365; p. 100 "Major, I am sorry." *LWTF*, 472; p. 100 "Even so, it was a lovely place and situation…" *LWTF*, 473; p. 101 "deep, deep pleasure.…The only pain was the knowledge…" *LWTF*, 478; p. 102 "A new and different hand was on the tiller." *LWTF*, 481; p. 103 "The time for negotiation has arrived." *LWTF*, 485; p. 103 "Our world had changed overnight…" *LWTF*, 485; p. 104 "sounded like some great herd of metallic beasts.…" *LWTF*, 490; p. 105 "I felt—even at the age of seventy-one…" *LWTF*, 491; p. 107 "You must be a very stupid old man." *MTAB*, 415; p. 107 "talk about negotiations on the one hand…" *LWTF*, 503; p. 108 "Take your guns, your knives, and your pangas…" *MTAB*, 431; p. 109 "Police Paid Inkatha to Block ANC." *MTAB*, 437; p. 110 "Ladies and gentlemen…" *MTAB*, 447; p. 111 "My patience snapped." *LWTF*, 526; p. 111 "He had been snatched away…" *LWTF*, 531; p. 113 "After nearly three hundred and fifty years…" *MTAB*, 482; p. 113 "I did not go into that voting station alone…" *LWTF*, 538; p. 114 "Today, all of us do, by our presence here…" From the Web site www.anc.org.za; p. 114 "We were taken from the bush…" *MTAB*, 486; p. 115 "That's what my bosses said." *MTAB*, 495; p. 115 "He took it like a chief." *MTAB*, 502; p. 115 "Our consensus speaks of the maturing of our young democracy.…" From the Web site www.anc.org.za; p. 117 "I invite you to join in the search for truth…" *MTAB*, 521; p. 117 "We must regard the healing of the South African nation as a process, not an event…" *MTAB*, 524; p. 118 "I look forward to that period when I will be able to wake up with the sun…" From the Web site www.anc.org.za; p. 119 "a proper example for the young people." *MTAB*, 540; p. 119 "The world needs symbols…" *MTAB*, 545; p. 119 "In every gnarly, knotted, distorted situation…" *MTAB*, 559

Index

For Further Study

Visit the About.com Web site on African history at www.africanhistory.about.com and have an expert answer all your questions about the history of South Africa.

Today, Robben Island is a museum. Visit it online at www.robben-island.org.za to learn more about the history of the island and Nelson Mandela's time there.

The African National Congress has an excellent Web site, including lots of information on its most famous leader. Go to www.anc.org.za/people/Mandela for dozens of links.

The Long Walk of Nelson Mandela, a documentary in the PBS television series Frontline, offers a fascinating look at Mandela's life and work. The Web site for the program, at www.pbs.org/wgbh/pages/frontline/shows/Mandela, includes extensive background material.

To find out about Mandela's current work, and to see the latest pictures of him, visit the Web site of the Nelson Mandela Foundation at www.nelsonmandela.org.

Acknowledgments

First and foremost, the authors would like to thank Alistair Boddy-Evans, the host of the remarkable About.com Web site on African history, www.africanhistory.about.com, and the expert vetter on our manuscript. Without Alistair's insightful comments and illuminating explanations, this book would not have been possible. We would also like to thank our editors at DK, Alisha Niehaus and John Searcy, as well as Beth Sutinis, Beth Hester, Anne Burns, and Tai Blanche for their help in making this project happen. And, for their patience, support, and forbearance, we would like to thank our children, Sophie, Irene, and Phoebe; Lenny's mother, Mella Hort; and our good friends Betti Cuomo, Linda Dorf (an admirer of Joe Slovo), Jackie Ching, and Joy Aquilino. Thank you all!

Picture Credits

About the Authors

Lenny Hort, the author of *George Washington* in the DK Biography series, has written many books for children, including the popular picture books *Did Dinosaurs Eat Pizza?* and *The Seals on the Bus*. His wife, Laaren Brown, has been a writer and editor for more than twenty years. They live in New Jersey with their daughters, Irene, Phoebe, and Sophie.

Other DK Biographies you may enjoy:

DK Biography: *Albert Einstein*
by Frieda Wishinsky
ISBN 0-7566-1247-0 paperback
ISBN 0-7566-1248-9 hardcover

DK Biography: *Harry Houdini*
by Vicki Cobb
ISBN 0-7566-1246-2 paperback
ISBN 0-7566-1245-4 hardcover

DK Biography: *Helen Keller*
by Leslie Garrett
ISBN 0-7566-0339-0 paperback
ISBN 0-7566-0488-5 hardcover

DK Biography: *Gandhi*
by Amy Pastan
ISBN 0-7566-2111-9 paperback
ISBN 0-7566-2112-7 hardcover

DK Biography: *John F. Kennedy*
by Howard S. Kaplan
ISBN 0-7566-0340-4 paperback
ISBN 0-7566-0489-3 hardcover

DK Biography: *Martin Luther King, Jr.*
by Amy Pastan
ISBN 0-7566-0342-0 paperback
ISBN 0-7566-0491-5 hardcover

DK Biography: *Abraham Lincoln*
by Tanya Lee Stone
ISBN 0-7566-0834-1 paperback
ISBN 0-7566-0833-3 hardcover

DK Biography: *Princess Diana*
by Joanne Mattern
ISBN 0-7566-1614-X paperback
ISBN 0-7566-1613-1 hardcover

DK Biography: *Eleanor Roosevelt*
by Kem Knapp Sawyer
ISBN 0-7566-1496-1 paperback
ISBN 0-7566-1495-3 hardcover

DK Biography: *George Washington*
by Lenny Hort
ISBN 0-7566-0835-X paperback
ISBN 0-7566-0832-5 hardcover

Look what the critics are saying about DK Biography!

"…highly readable, worthwhile overviews for young people…"—*Booklist*

"This new series from the inimitable DK Publishing brings together the usual brilliant photography with a historian's approach to biography subjects."
—*Ingram Library Services*